real world micro

FOURTH EDITION

Edited by
RANDY ALBELDA, ROSE BATT,
BETSY REED, CHRIS TILLY, AND THE
DOLLARS & SENSE COLLECTIVE

REAL WORLD MICRO, FOURTH EDITION

ISBN: 1-878585-32-0

Published by
Dollars & Sense
Economic Affairs Bureau, Inc.
One Summer Street
Somerville, MA 02143
(617) 628-8411

Real World Micro is edited by the *Dollars & Sense* Collective, publishers of *Dollars & Sense* magazine and annual editions of *Real World Micro*, *Real World Macro*, and *Real World Banking*.

The 1993 collective:
Randy Albelda, Rose Batt, Mark Breibart, Marc Breslow, Laurie Dougherty, Debbie Dover, Amy Gluckman, Patricia Horn, David Levy, Dalya Massachi, Gretchen McClean, John Miller, Betsy Reed, Rich Rosen, Susan Schacht, Brian Snyder, John Stamm, Chris Tilly, Stuart Wamsley.

Cover Art and Design: Nick Thorkelson
Production: Patricia Horn, Sheila Walsh

Printed by:
Banta Co.
Curtis Reed Plaza
P.O. Box 60
Menasha, WI 54952

Table of Contents

Introduction

According to traditional microeconomic theory, the market system provides the best of all possible worlds, a world in which consumers get exactly what they want (given their budgets, of course), and firms produce the most socially desirable kind and amount of goods (while making money at the same time). Our collection of articles challenges this rosy picture of the world and the assumptions behind it. In our view, the free-market system produces neither the best nor the fairest results for the majority of people—both in the United States and elsewhere.

The fourth edition of *Real World Micro* contains 31 articles that have appeared in *Dollars & Sense*, a monthly economic affairs magazine. Together, they present an alternative vision of how markets work—a vision based on real markets, real people, and real government programs.

The first section critically examines some basic microeconomic concepts, like the "invisible hand" and market power. "The Gospel of Free Trade" examines the ideology of free trade, assessing its implications for different countries and populations.

The second section, "Real World Markets," offers an alternative look at the world of supply and demand. Traditional microeconomics disposes of the hard questions in this area by *assuming* that markets naturally tend toward equilibrium. In the real world, such balance is not always attainable or even desirable. The articles in this section look at how and where shortages occur, when price controls work best, and how supply and demand interact in real markets.

Much of traditional microeconomics curriculum is devoted to consumers, who account for the bulk of spending in the economy. In most microeconomic theory, consumers are assumed to have complete and perfect information about both their own economic resources and the products they buy. Both assumptions are fallacious. The third chapter examines the ways in which consumers' choices are constrained by their resources or dominated by external forces, most notably advertising.

Microeconomics treats firms as profit-maximizing enterprises. This is one assumption the editors of *Dollars & Sense* don't challenge. However, unlike most microeconomics textbooks, the articles in the fourth chapter of *Real World Micro* argue that profit maximization can be dangerous to your health—and to the overall health of the economy. In this chapter, we look at industries and examine how, in the real world, different market structures—monopoly, oligopoly, and competition—play out. In "Who Owns the Government," we also reveal the ways in which companies—and individuals—buy federal government favors.

The fifth chapter covers labor markets, which differ significantly from the markets for pizzas, haircuts, airplanes, or other goods. Labor is an input, a service or product that firms purchase in order to produce their goods. Unlike other factors of production, though, labor is a human input. If workers don't work, they don't get paid. If workers don't get paid, they suffer, their families suffer, and the economy suffers because workers cannot buy all the goods that are produced. Articles in this section discuss why labor markets fail to generate full employment, why workers can't always earn a living from the wages they command, and how discrimination (by age, race, or sex) distorts the opportunities available to workers.

The sixth chapter discusses what happens when the market doesn't work. Articles examine some of the goods the private sector has failed to provide adequately, such as health care in the United States. We also show how work effort is not always the principal determinant of economic well-being and how inequality has risen in the United States.

Our anthology would be incomplete without readings on the global economy. The final chapter examines the North American Free Trade Agreement, assesses the failure of central planning in the Soviet Union, and evaluates different perspectives on international competitiveness.

While *Real World Micro* does not represent a complete critique of traditional microeconomic theory, we hope it will inject an element of realism into your understanding of the market system. We welcome your comments and suggestions for future editions.

—The Editors of *Dollars & Sense* Magazine

The Basics

Dollars & Sense, November 1989

Shaking the Invisible Hand

The uncertain foundations of free-market economics

By Chris Tilly

> *"It is not from the benevolence of the butcher, the brewer or the baker that we expect our dinner, but from their regard to their own interest...[No individual] intends to promote the public interest... [rather, he is] led by an invisible hand to promote an end which was no part of his intention."*
>
> Adam Smith,
> *The Wealth of Nations*, 1776

Seen the Invisible Hand lately? It's all around us these days, propping up conservative arguments in favor of free trade, deregulation, and tax-cutting.

Today's advocates for "free," competitive markets echo Adam Smith's claim that unfettered markets translate the self-

---

CHRIS TILLY, a member of the *Dollars & Sense* Collective, teaches urban planning at the University of Lowell in Massachusetts.

ish pursuit of individual gain into the greatest benefit for all. They trumpet the superiority of capitalist free enterprise over socialist efforts to supplant the market with a planned economy, and even decry liberal attempts to moderate the market. Anything short of competitive markets, they proclaim, yields economic inefficiency, making society worse off.

But the economic principle underlying this fanfare is shaky indeed. Since the late 19th century, mainstream economists have struggled to prove that Smith was right—that the chaos of free markets leads to a blissful economic order. In the 1950s, U.S. economists Kenneth Arrow and Gerard Debreu finally came up with a theoretical proof, which many orthodox economists view as the centerpiece of modern economic theory.

Although this proof is the product of the best minds of mainstream economics, it ends up saying surprisingly little in defense of free markets. The modern

theory of the Invisible Hand shows that given certain assumptions, free markets reduce the wasteful use of economic resources—but perpetuate unequal income distribution.

To prove free markets cut waste, economists must make a number of farfetched assumptions: there are no concentrations of economic power; buyers and sellers know every detail about the present and future economy; and all costs of production are borne by producers while all benefits from consumption are paid for by consumers (see box for a complete list). Take away any one of these assumptions and markets can lead to stagnation, recession, and other forms of waste—as in fact they do.

In short, the economic theory invoked by conservatives to justify free markets instead starkly reveals their limitations.

THE FRUITS OF FREE MARKETS

The basic idea behind the Invisible Hand can be illustrated with a story. Suppose that I grow apples and you grow oranges. We both grow tired of eating the same fruit all the time and decide to trade. Perhaps we start by trading one apple for one orange. This exchange satisfies both of us, because in fact I would gladly give up more than one apple to get an orange, and you would readily pay more than one orange for an apple. And as long as swapping one more apple for one more orange makes us both better off, we will continue to trade.

Eventually, the trading will come to a stop. I begin to notice that the novelty of oranges wears off as I accumulate a larger pile of them and the apples I once had a surplus of become more precious to me as they grow scarcer. At some point, I draw the line: in order to obtain one more apple from me, you must give me more than one orange. But your remaining oranges have also become more valuable to you. Up to now, each successive trade has made both of us better off. Now there is no further exchange that benefits us both, so we agree to stop trading until the next crop comes in.

Note several features of this parable. Both you and I end up happier by trading freely. If the government stepped in and limited fruit trading, neither of us would be as well off. In fact, the government cannot do anything in the apple/orange market that will make both of us better off than does the free market.

Adding more economic actors, products, money, and costly production processes complicates the picture, but we reach the same conclusions. Most of us sell our labor time in the market rather than fruit; we sell it for money that we then use to buy apples, oranges, and whatever else we need. The theory of the Invisible Hand tells us a trip to the fruit stand improves the lot of both consumer and seller; likewise, the sale of labor time benefits both employer and employee. What's more, according to the theory, competition between apple farmers insures that consumers will get apples produced at the lowest possible cost. Government intervention still can only make things worse.

This fable provides a ready-made policy guide. Substitute "Japanese autos" and "U.S. agricultural products" for apples and oranges, and the fable tells you that import quotas or tariffs only make the people of both countries worse off. Change the industries to airlines or telephone services, and the fable calls for deregulation. Or re-tell the tale in the labor market: minimum wages and unions (which prevent workers from individually bargaining over their wages) hurt employers and workers.

FRUIT SALAD

Unfortunately for free-market boosters, two major shortcomings make a fruit salad out of this story. First, even if free markets perform as advertised, they deliver only one benefit—the prevention of certain economically wasteful practices—while preserving inequality. According to the theory, competitive markets wipe out two kinds of waste: unrealized trades and

inefficient production. Given the right assumptions, markets ensure that when two parties both stand to gain from a trade, they make that trade, as in the apples-and-oranges story. Competition compels producers to search for the most efficient, lowest-cost production methods—again, given the right preconditions.

Though eliminating waste is a worthy goal, it leaves economic inequality untouched. Returning once more to the orchard, if I start out with all of the apples and oranges and you start out with none, that situation is free of waste: no swap can make us both better off since you have nothing to trade! Orthodox economists acknowledge that even in the ideal competitive market, those who start out rich stay rich, while the poor remain poor. Many of them argue that attempts at redistributing income will most certainly create economic inefficiencies, justifying the preservation of current inequities.

But in real-life economics, competition does lead to waste. Companies wastefully duplicate each other's research and build excess productive capacity. Cost-cutting often leads to shoddy products, worker speedup, and unsafe working conditions. People and factories stand

idle while houses go unbuilt and people go unfed. That's because of the second major problem: Real economies don't match the assumptions of the Invisible Hand theory.

Of course, all economic theories build their arguments on a set of simplifying assumptions about the world. These assumptions often sacrifice some less important aspects of reality in order to focus on the economic mechanisms of interest. But in the case of the Invisible Hand, the theoretical preconditions contradict several central features of the economy.

For one thing, markets are only guaranteed to prevent waste if the economy runs on "perfect competition": individual sellers compete by cutting prices, individual buyers compete by raising price offers, and nobody holds concentrated economic power. But today's giant corporations hardly match this description. Coke and Pepsi compete with advertising rather than price cuts. The oil companies keep prices high enough to register massive profits every year. Employers coordinate the pay and benefits they offer to avoid bidding up compensation. Workers, in turn, marshal their own forces via unionization—another depar-

ture from perfect competition.

Indeed, the jargon of "perfect competition" overlooks the fact that property ownership itself confers disproportionate economic power. "In the competitive model," orthodox economist Paul Samuelson commented, "it makes no difference whether capital hires labor or the other way around." He argued that given perfect competition among workers and among capitalists, wages and profits would remain the same regardless of who does the hiring. But unemployment—a persistent feature of market-driven economies—makes job loss very costly to workers. The sting my boss feels when I "fire" him by quitting my job hardly equals the setback I experience when he fires me.

PERFECT INFORMATION?

In addition, the grip of the Invisible Hand is only sure if all buyers and sellers have "perfect information" about the present and future state of markets. In the present, this implies consumers know exactly what they are buying—an assumption hard to swallow in these days of alar-laden apples and chicken a la Salmonella. Employers must know exactly what skills workers have and how hard they will work—suppositions any real-life manager would laugh at.

Perfect information also means sellers can always sniff out unsatisfied demands, and buyers can detect any excess supplies of goods. Orthodox economists rely on the metaphor of an omnipresent "auctioneer" who is always calling out prices so all buyers and sellers can find mutually agreeable prices and consummate every possible sale. But in the actual economy, the auctioneer is nowhere to be found, and markets are plagued by surpluses and shortages.

Perfect information about the future is even harder to come by. For example, a company decides whether or not to build a new plant based on whether it expects sales to rise. But predicting future demand is a tricky matter. One reason is that people may save money today in order to buy (demand) goods and services in the future. The problem comes in predicting when. As economist John Maynard Keynes observed in 1934, "An act of individual saving means—so to speak—a decision not to have dinner

Assumptions and reality

The claim that free markets lead to efficiency and reduced waste rests on seven main assumptions. However, these assumptions differ sharply from economic reality. (Assumptions 1, 3, 4, and are discussed in more detail in the article.)

ASSUMPTION ONE: No market power. No individual buyer or seller, nor any group of buyers or sellers, has the power to affect the market-wide level of prices, wages, or profits.

REALITY ONE: Our economy is dotted with centers of market power, from large corporations to unions. Furthermore, employers have an edge in bargaining with workers because of the threat of unemployment.

ASSUMPTION TWO: No economies of scale. Small plants can produce as cheaply as large ones.

REALITY TWO: In fields such as mass-production industry, transportation, communications, and agriculture, large producers enjoy a cost advantage, limiting competition.

ASSUMPTION THREE: Perfect information about the present. Buyers and sellers know everything there is to know about the goods being exchanged. Also, each is aware of the wishes of every other potential buyer and seller in the market.

REALITY THREE: The world is full of lemons—goods about which the buyer is inadequately informed. Also, people are not mind-

readers, so sellers get stuck with surpluses and willing buyers are unable to find the products they want.

ASSUMPTION FOUR: Perfect information about the future. Contracts between buyers and sellers cover every possible future eventuality.

REALITY FOUR: Uncertainty clouds the future of any economy. Futures markets are limited.

ASSUMPTION FIVE: You only get what you pay for. Nobody can impose a cost on somebody else, nor obtain a benefit from them, without paying.

REALITY FIVE: In a free market, polluters can impose costs on the rest of us without paying. And when a public good like a park is built or roads are maintained, everyone benefits whether or not they helped to pay for it.

ASSUMPTION SIX: Self-interest. In economic matters, each person cares only about his or her own level of well-being.

REALITY SIX: Solidarity, jealousy, and even love for one's family violate this assumption.

ASSUMPTION SEVEN: No joint production. Each production process has only one product.

REALITY SEVEN: Even in an age of specialization, there are plenty of exceptions to this rule. For example, large service firms such as hospitals or universities produce a variety of different services using the same resources.

today. But it does not necessitate a decision to have dinner or to buy a pair of boots a week hence...or to consume any specified thing at any specified date. Thus it depresses the business of preparing today's dinner without stimulating the business of making ready for some future act of consumption." Keynes concluded that far from curtailing waste, free

markets gave rise to the colossal waste of human and economic resources that was the Great Depression—in part because of this type of uncertainty about the future.

FREE LUNCH

The dexterity of the Invisible Hand also depends on the principle that "You only get what you pay for." This "no free lunch" principle seems at first glance a reasonable description of the economy. But major exceptions arise. One is what economists call "externalities"—economic transactions that take place outside the market. Consider a hospital that dumps syringes at sea. In effect, the hospital gets a free lunch by passing the costs of waste disposal on to the rest of us. Because no market exists where the right to dump is bought and sold, free markets do nothing to compel the hospital to bear the costs of dumping—which is why the government must step in.

Public goods such as sewer systems also violate the "no free lunch" rule. Once the sewer system is in place, everyone shares in the benefits of the waste disposal, regardless of whether or not they helped pay for it. Suppose sewer systems were sold in a free market, in which each person had the opportunity to buy an individual share. Then any sensible, self-interested consumer would hold back from buying his or her fair share—and wait for others to provide the service. This irrational situation would persist unless consumers could somehow collectively agree on how extensive a sewer system to produce—once more bringing government into the picture.

Most orthodox economists claim that the list of externalities and public goods in the economy is short and easily addressed. Liberals and radicals, on the other hand, offer a long list: for example, public goods include education, health care, and decent public transportation—all in short supply in our society.

Because real markets deviate from the ideal markets envisioned in the theory of the Invisible Hand, they give us both inequality and waste. But if the theory is so far off the mark, why do mainstream economists and policy-makers place so much stock in it? They fundamentally believe the profit motive is the best guide for the economy. If you believe that "What's good for General Motors is good for the USA," the Invisible Hand theory can seem quite reasonable. Business interests, government, and the media constantly reinforce this belief, and reward those who can dress it up in theoretical terms. As long as capital remains the dominant force in society, the Invisible Hand will maintain its grip on the hearts and minds of us all. ■

Dollars & Sense, July/August 1989

Choose Your Poison

Competition and concentration are both integral to capitalism, but both have their drawbacks

By Thea Lee

According to an old joke, if you lined up all the economists in the world end to end, they couldn't reach a conclusion. In some cases, that may not be such a bad thing. Take the case of the classic and unresolved debate among mainstream economists over whether the U.S. economy suffers from too much competition, or too little.

Though the debate is somewhat arcane, it has significance outside economists' ivory towers. After all, many products labeled "Made in the USA" are also labeled overpriced, poor quality, and technologically outmoded by U.S. consumers. Some experts respond to U.S. decline with calls for greater competition, to get complacent corporate fat-cats off their duffs. Others say U.S. firms are competing too hard, pointing to Japan, where the government encourages cooperation and monopolization.

What the debate misses, of course, is that in the end there is little choice at all. When it comes to capitalism, what you see is what we've got.

BEATING THE COMPETITION

Still, from the halls of academia to the shores of the Potomac, that is the choice they pose: competition, narrowly defined, or concentration. By competition

they mean something akin to what introductory textbooks call "perfect competition": many small firms selling a standardized product using identical or similar technology. Concentration refers to domination of a market by one or several large firms.

U.S. industries today run the gamut from extremely concentrated to fairly competitive. Economists consider an industry concentrated when its top four companies account for more than 40% of total sales in the industry. On one end of the spectrum are the aircraft and breakfast cereal industries, where four or five firms account for most U.S. production. No market comes close to meeting the textbook specifications for perfect competition, but one can still find industries in which a large number of producers compete for sales. The clothing and machine tool industries, for example, remain relatively competitive. By these standards, about one-third of U.S. goods are manufactured in concentrated industries, about one fifth are made in competitive industries, and the rest fall somewhere in between.

PROS AND CONS

Those who tout the benefits of competition make a broad range of claims on its behalf. In addition to keeping prices low, they say the quality of the product is constantly improving, as companies seek a competitive edge. That same desire, they claim, drives firms toward techno-

THEA LEE is a *Dollars & Sense* editor.

logical innovations, leading to productivity increases.

The story, of course, is not so simple. Prices indeed remain low, but so do wages and profits. Firms tend to go bankrupt fairly often, since they operate so close to the edge of solvency. The Dickensian factories during England's Industrial Revolution and New York's sweatshops are both examples of how competition looks outside of the textbooks. All in all, it's a brutal system, and most businesses devote a lot of energy trying to shield themselves from its rigors.

For companies in very competitive markets, the same "whip of competition" that keeps prices down undermines many of competition's other supposed benefits. The flurry of competition in the airline industry following deregulation, for example, hardly resulted in a higher quality product. Flying became temporarily cheaper, but also less comfortable, reliable, and safe.

Technological innovation from competition is also more myth than reality.

All in all, competition is a brutal system and most businesses devote a lot of energy trying to shield themselves from its rigors.

Who competes, who doesn't

Industry	Percent of sales by top four firms
Cereal breakfast foods	86
Greeting card publishing	84
Aircraft	64
Soaps and other detergents	60
Farm machinery and equipment	53
Cement, hydraulic	31
Machine tools, metal-cutting types	30
Women's and misses' dresses	6
Wood pallet skids	5

Source: *1982 Census of Manufacturers,* 1986

Small firms in competitive industries do very little research and development. They lack both the cash needed to make long-term investments and the market power to guarantee a return on that investment. Agriculture may be the exception that proves the rule. That highly competitive industry has made marked productivity gains, but its research is supported by the taxpayer, and its risks are reduced by government price supports.

Of course, the biggest myth about competition is that it is in any way a "natural state" for capitalism. In the somewhat surreal world inhabited by mainstream economists, there are few cost advantages to being large, and in most industries, newcomers can easily enter the industry and compete. In fact, in most markets the very process of competing for high profits or a bigger market share tends to create a concentrated, rather than a competitive, market structure.

This process occurs in several ways. Big firms sometimes drive their smaller competitors out of business by selectively cutting prices to the bone. The smaller firms may lack the immediately available financial resources to last out the low prices. In the 1960s, several of IBM's smaller competitors sued it for cutting prices in a pattern that was designed to drive the smaller firms out of the market.

Other firms eliminate competitors by buying them out—either in a hostile takeover or a friendly merger. Either way, a former competitor is neutralized. This strategy used to be severely limited by strict antitrust guidelines that prohibited most horizontal mergers—those between two firms that formerly competed in the same market. The Reagan administration's corporate lapdogs at the Justice Department, however, loosened the merger guidelines significantly in the early 1980s. Since that time, many large mergers between former competitors have been allowed to go through, most notably in the airline industry.

THE POWER OF CONCENTRATION

Concentration, then, is as natural to capitalism as competition. And its evils are perhaps more well known.

Corporations in industries where there are few competitors may compete, but their competitive tension is seldom channeled into prolonged price wars. The soft drink industry is a classic example. Coke and Pepsi introduce new drinks and mount massive ad campaigns to win market share, but the net result is not lower prices. In fact, because competition between industry giants tends to be based more on product differentiation than price, companies pass on their inflated advertising expenses to consumers. In the highly concentrated breakfast cereal market, the package frequently costs more than the contents. And of every dollar you pay for a box, nearly 20 cents goes for advertising.

While firms in concentrated industries tend to have the resources to innovate, competition-advocates' charges of corporate complacency are on the money. The steel industry illustrates the point. A few major producers earned steady profits through the 1950s and 1960s but were caught off-guard when new technologies vaulted foreign steelmakers to the top of the industry in the 1970s.

When IBM dominated the computer industry in the 1960s and early 1970s, innovation proceeded quite slowly, particularly compared to the frantic scramble in that industry today. With no competitors to worry about, it was more profitable for IBM to sit tight, since innovation would only have made its own machines obsolete.

But it takes resources to develop and market a new idea, which gives large corporations distinct advantages. The original idea for the photocopier may have come from a patent lawyer who worked nights in his basement, but Xerox spent $16 million before it had a product it could sell. RCA invested $65 million developing the color television. RCA could take this gamble because its dominance in the television market ensured that it would not be immediately undercut by some other firm.

Such market power is a double-edged sword for these firms' workers. In prosperous times, companies are able to grant workers higher wages, knowing they can then pass the higher costs on to consumers. The strongest unions and best paid workers have historically been in industries where a few firms controlled large shares of their markets—auto, steel, and tires, for example. In their heyday, companies in these industries could well afford yearly wage and benefit increases.

When profits are threatened, though, firms in concentrated markets also have more resources with which to fight labor. They are better able to weather a strike, oppose unionization, and make agreements with rivals not to take advantage of each other's labor troubles.

CONCENTRATION OR CONGLOMERATION?

What is oddest about the debate over competition and concentration is how little it has to do with the real world—and the choices open to policy-makers. In the last couple of decades, the overall level of concentration in the economy has increased only slightly. As older industries become more concentrated, newer, more competitive ones crop up, leaving overall concentration steady.

Conglomeration is a different matter, however. Corporate ownership of assets has become much more concentrated over time, reflecting the rise in conglomerates—corporations doing business in a variety of industries. Four decades ago, the top 200 firms accounted for 48% of all sales and 30% of all manufacturing

value added in the U.S. economy. By the early 1980s, the 200 biggest firms controlled 60% of sales and over 40% of value added.

Most mainstream economists see these groupings as irrelevant for the competitive structure of the economy. Antitrust laws place no restrictions on firms from different industries banding together under one corporate roof. But sheer size can easily affect competition in the markets of the individual firms involved. A parent company can use one especially profitable subsidiary to subsidize some of the start-up costs for a new venture, giving it a competitive edge. And

if one board of directors controls major interests in related industries, it can obviously influence any of those markets more forcefully.

Such may be the case if the proposed merger of Time Inc. and Warner Communications is okayed by the feds. The resulting conglomerate, Time Warner Inc., would control massive sections of the home entertainment business, bringing together Time's journalists, film and television producers, and authors and Warner's entertainment machine, which includes Home Box Office, the nation's largest pay television channel. The conglomerate will then be able to influence the entertainment business from the initial point—the actors, writers, and directors—up to the point where the finished products appear on people's televisions via cable.

Conglomerates or large concentrated firms also wield disproportionate political power, since their size alone allows them to maintain paid lobbyists in Washington. They can use this political clout to push through legislation that gives their subsidiary firms an edge in their individual markets.

CHOOSE YOUR POISON

Competition, concentration, or conglomeration: The choice is an unsavory one indeed. Opting for lots of tiny, competing firms leaves labor squeezed and sacrifices the potential technological advantages that come with concentrated resources. Yet the big monopolies tend to dominate their markets, charge high

prices, and waste countless resources on glitzy ad campaigns and trivial product differentiation. And the big conglomerate firms, while not necessarily dominant in any single market, wield a frightening amount of political and economic power, with budgets larger than those of some countries.

Of course, in the end there is nothing to choose, and capitalism continues to stumble along. New competitive industries will tend to get more concentrated over time. Companies in both competitive and concentrated industries will tend to merge with firms in other industries. And we're left with the continuing shake-out of capitalism leading toward conglomeration.

And, like so much that passes for economic debate in the United States, we are rarely told of what may be the most attractive choice of all: "none of the above." ∎

> Like so much that passes for economic debate in the United States, we are rarely told of what may be the most attractive choice of all: "none of the above."

Dollars & Sense, November 1991

The Gospel of Free Trade

A heretical view

By Arthur MacEwan

Free trade! It's the cure-all for the 1990s. With all the zeal of Christian missionaries, the U.S. government has been preaching, advocating, pushing, and coercing around the globe for "free trade."

While a Mexico-U.S.-Canada free trade pact is the immediate aim of U.S. policy, George Bush has heralded a future free trade zone from the northern coast of Canada to the southern tip of Chile. For Eastern Europe, U.S. advisers prescribe unfettered capitalism and ridicule as unworkable any move toward a "third way." Wherever any modicum of economic success appears in the Third World, free traders extol it as one more example of their program's wonders.

Free traders also praise their gospel as the proper policy at home. The path to true salvation—or economic expansion, which, in this day and age, seems to be the same thing—lies in opening our markets to foreign goods. Get rid of trade barriers, allow business to go where it wants and do what it wants. We will all get rich.

Yet the history of the United States and other advanced capitalist countries teaches us that virtually all advanced capitalist countries found economic success in protectionism, not in free trade. Likewise, heavy government intervention has characterized those cases of rapid and sustained economic growth in the Third World.

Free trade, does, however, have its uses. Highly developed nations can use free trade to extend their power and their control of the world's wealth, and business can use it as a weapon against labor. Most important, free trade can limit efforts to redistribute income more equally, undermine progressive social programs, and keep people from democratically controlling their economic lives.

A DAY IN THE PARK

At the beginning of the nineteenth century, Lowell, Massachusetts, became the premier site of the country's textile industry. Today, thanks to the Lowell National Historical Park, you can tour the huge mills, ride through the canals that redirected the Merrimack River's power to the mills, and learn the story of the textile workers, from the Yankee "mill girls" of the 1820s through the various waves of immigrant laborers who poured into the city over the next century.

During a day in the park, visitors get a graphic picture of the importance of nineteenth century industry to the later economic growth and prosperity of the United States. Lowell and the other mill towns of the era were centers of growth. They not only created a demand for Southern cotton, they also created a demand for new machinery, maintenance of old machinery, parts, dyes, skills, construction materials, construction machinery, more skills, equipment to move the raw materials and products, parts and maintenance for that equipment, and still more skills. The mill towns also created markets—concentrated groups of wage earners who needed to buy products to sustain themselves. As centers of economic activity, Lowell and similar mill towns contributed to U.S. economic growth far beyond the value of the textiles they produced.

The U.S. textile industry emerged decades after the industrial revolution had spawned Britain's powerful textile industry. Nonetheless, it survived and prospered. British linens inundated markets throughout the world in the early nineteenth century, as the British navy nurtured free trade and kept ports open for commerce. In the United States, however, hostilities leading up to the War of 1812 and then a substantial tariff made British textiles relatively expensive. These limitations on trade allowed the Lowell mills to prosper, acting as a catalyst for other industries and helping to create the skilled work force at the center of U.S. economic expansion.

Beyond textiles, however, tariffs did not play a great role in the United States during the early nineteenth century. Southern planters had considerable power, and while they were willing to make some compromises, they opposed protecting manufacturing in general because that protection forced up the price of the goods they purchased with their cotton revenues. The Civil War wiped out Southern opposition to protectionism, and from the 1860s through World War I, U.S. industry prospered behind considerable tariff barriers.

ARTHUR MacEWAN, a *Dollars &Sense* founder, teaches economics at the University of Massachusetts at Boston.

Virtually all advanced capitalist countries found economic success in protectionism.

DIFFERENT COUNTRIES, SIMILAR STORIES

The story of the importance of protectionism in bringing economic growth has been repeated, with local variations, in almost all other advanced capitalist countries. During the late nineteenth century, Germany entered the major league of international economic powers with substantial protection and government support for its industries. Likewise, in nineteenth century France and Italy, national consolidation behind protectionist barriers was a key to economic development.

Only Britain—which entered the industrial era first—might be touted as an example of successful development without tariff protection. Yet, in addition to starting first, Britain built its industry through the expansion of its empire and the British navy, hardly prime ingredients in any recipe for free trade.

Japan provides a particularly important case of successful government protection and support for industrial development. In the post-World War II era, when the Japanese established the foundations for the modern "miracle," the government rejected free trade and extensive foreign investment and instead promoted its national firms.

In the 1950s, for example, the government protected the country's fledgling auto firms from foreign competition. At first, quotas limited imports to $500,000 (in current dollars) each year; in the 1960s, prohibitively high tariffs replaced the quotas. Furthermore, the Japanese allowed foreign investment only insofar as it contributed to developing domestic industry. The government encouraged Japanese companies to import foreign technology, but required them to produce 90% of parts domestically within five years.

The Japanese also protected their computer industry. In the early 1970s, as the industry was developing, companies and individuals could only purchase a foreign machine if a suitable Japanese model was not available. IBM was allowed to produce within the country, but only when it licensed basic patents to Japanese firms. And IBM computers produced in Japan were treated as foreign-made machines.

Today, while Japan towers as the world's most dynamic industrial and financial power, one looks in vain for the role free trade played in its success. The Japanese government provided an effective framework, support, and protection for the country's capitalist development.

Likewise, in the Third World, capitalism has generated high rates of economic growth where government involvement, and not free trade, played the central role. South Korea is the most striking case. "Korea is an example of a country that grew very fast and yet violated the canons of conventional economic wisdom," writes Alice Amsden, in *Asia's Next Giant: South Korea and Late Industrialization*, widely acclaimed as the most important recent book on the Korean economy. "In Korea, instead of the market mechanism allocating resources and guiding private entrepreneurship, the government made most of the pivotal investment decisions. Instead of firms operating in a competitive market structure, they each operated with an extraordinary degree of market control, protected from foreign competition."

With Mexico, three recent years of relatively moderate growth, about 3%-4% per year, have led the purveyors of free trade to claim it as one of their success stories. Yet Mexico has been opening its economy increasingly since the early 1980s, and most of the decade was an utter disaster. Even if the 1980s are written off as the cost of transition, the recent "success" does not compare well with what Mexico achieved in the era when its government intervened heavily in the economy and protected national industry. From 1940 to 1980, with policies of state-led economic development and extensive limits on imports, Mexican national output grew at the high rate of about 6% per year.

The recent Mexican experience does put to rest any ideas that free market policies will improve the living conditions for the masses of the people in the Third World. The Mexican government has paved the road for free trade policies by reducing or eliminating social welfare programs. In addition, between 1976 and 1990, the real minimum wage declined by 60%. Mexico's increasing orientation toward foreign trade has also destroyed the country's self-sufficiency in food, and the influx of foreign food grains has forced small farmers off the land and into the ranks of the urban unemployed.

THE USES OF FREE TRADE

While free trade is not the best economic growth or development policy, the largest and most powerful firms in many countries find it highly profitable. As Britain led the cheers for free trade in the early nineteenth century, when its own industry was firmly established, so the United States—or at least many firms based in the United States—finds it a profitable policy in the late twentieth century.

For U.S. firms, access to foreign markets is a high priority. Mexico may be relatively poor, but with a population of 85 million it provides a substantial market. Furthermore, Mexican labor is cheap; using modern production techniques, Mexican workers can be as productive as workers in the United States. For U.S. firms to obtain full access to the Mexican market, the United States must open its borders to Mexican goods. Also, if U.S. firms are to take full advantage of cheap foreign labor and sell the goods produced abroad to U.S. consumers, the United States must be open to imports.

On the other side of the border, wealthy Mexicans face a choice between advancing their interests through national development or advancing their interests through ties to U.S. firms and access to U.S. markets. For many years, they chose the former route. This led to some development of the Mexican economy but also—due to corruption and the massive power of the ruling party—created huge concentrations of wealth in the hands of a few small groups of firms and individuals. Eventually, these groups came into conflict with their own government over regulation and taxation. Having benefited from government largess, they now see their fortunes in greater freedom from government control and, particularly, in greater access to foreign markets and partnerships with large foreign companies. National development is a secondary concern when more involvement with international commerce will produce greater riches quicker.

In addition, the old program of state-led development in Mexico ran into severe problems. These problems came to the surface in the 1980s with the international debt crisis. Owing huge amounts

For any economy to operate in the interests of the great majority, people's conscious choices must command the economy.

of money to foreign banks, the Mexican government was forced to respond to pressure from the International Monetary Fund, the U.S. government, and large international banks. That pressure meshed with the pressure coming from Mexico's own richest elites, and the result has been the move toward free trade and a greater opening of the Mexican economy to foreign investment.

Of course, in the United States, Mexico, and elsewhere, advocates of free trade claim that their policies are in everyone's interest. Free trade, they point out, will mean cheaper products for all. Consumers in the United States, who are mostly workers, will be richer because their wages will buy more. In both Mexico and the United States, they argue, rising trade will create more jobs. If some workers lose their jobs because cheaper imported goods are available, export industries will produce new ones.

Such arguments obscure many of the most important issues in the free trade debate. Stated, as they usually are, as universal truths, these arguments are just plain silly. No one, for example, touring the Lowell National Historical Park could seriously argue that people in the United States would have been better off had there been no tariff on textiles. Yes, in 1820, they could have purchased textile goods more cheaply, but the cost would have been an industrially backward, impoverished nation. One could make the same point with the Japanese auto and computer industries, or indeed with numerous other examples from the last two centuries of capitalist development.

In the modern era, even though the United States already has a relatively developed economy with highly skilled workers, a freely open international economy does not serve the interests of U.S. workers, though it will benefit large firms. U.S. workers today are in competition with workers around the globe. Many different workers in many different places can produce the same goods and services. Thus, an international economy governed by the free trade agenda will bring down wages for U.S. workers.

The problem is not simply that of workers in a few industries—such as auto and steel—where import competition is the most obvious and immediate problem. A country's openness to the international economy affects the entire structure of earnings in that country. Free trade forces down the general level of wages across the board, even of those workers not directly affected by imports. The simple fact is that when companies can produce the same products in several different places, it is owners who gain because they can move their factories and funds around much more easily than workers can move themselves around. Capital is mobile, labor is much less mobile. Businesses, not workers, gain from having a larger territory in which to roam.

THE WEAPON OF FREE TRADE

But the difficulties with free trade do not end with wages. Free trade is a weapon in the hands of business when it opposes any progressive social programs. Efforts to place environmental restrictions on firms are met with the threat of moving production abroad. Higher taxes to improve the schools? Business threatens to go elsewhere. Better health and safety regulations? The same response.

Some might argue that the losses from free trade for people in the United States will be balanced by gains for most people in poor countries—lower wages in the United States, but higher wages in Mexico. Free trade, then, would bring about international equality. Not likely. In fact, as pointed out above, free trade reforms in Mexico have helped force down wages and reduce social welfare programs, processes rationalized by efforts to make Mexican goods competitive on international markets.

Gains for Mexican workers, like those for U.S. workers, depend on their power in relation to business. Free trade and the imperative of international "competitiveness" are just as much weapons in the hands of firms operating in Mexico as they are for firms operating in the United States. The great mobility of capital is business' best trump card in dealing with labor and popular demands for social change—in the United States, Mexico, and elsewhere.

None of this means that people should demand that their economies operate as fortresses, protected from all foreign economic incursions. There are great gains that can be obtained from international economic relations—when a nation manages those relations in the interests of the great majority of the people. Protectionism often simply supports narrow vested interests, corrupt officials, and wealthy industrialists. In rejecting free trade, we should move beyond traditional protectionism.

Yet, at this time, rejecting free trade is an essential first step. Free trade places all the cards in the hands of business. More than ever, free trade would subject us to the "bottom line," or at least the bottom line as calculated by those who own and run large companies.

For any economy to operate in the interest of the great majority, people's conscious choices—about the environment, income distribution, safety, and health—must command the economy. The politics of democratic decision-making must control business. In today's world, politics operates primarily on a national level. To give up control over our national economy—as does any people that accepts free trade—is to give up control over our economic lives. ∎

RESOURCES: *NACLA's Report on the Americas*, Vol. XXIV, No. 6, May 1991, "The New Gospel: North American Free Trade"; Robert Pollin, Alexander Cockburn, "Capitalism and its Specters: The World, the Free Market and the Left," *The Nation*, February 25, 1991; P. Armstrong, A. Glyn, J. Harrison, *Capitalism Since World War II*, 1984.

Dollars & Sense, July/August 1992

Markets & Socialism

Markets aren't just for capitalism anymore

By Tom Weisskopf

What kind of economic system can best foster equality, democracy, and solidarity? To champions of capitalism, the unraveling of the Soviet-bloc economies proves socialism is no longer a contender. But to the left, much of which has denounced these societies for decades, the breakdown of the old order clears the way for a truly socialist vision.

Two pictures prevail. One draws on the liberal-democratic tradition, and holds that any socialist society worthy of the name must rest on democratic elections and a constitution that protects civil rights and liberties. Liberal-democratic socialists would reform the political institutions associated with Western capitalism rather than discard them, making them more genuinely democratic and extending them from the political to the social and economic arenas. Collective ownership would replace private ownership of enterprise. But the market, shaped by government, would remain a basic fixture of the economy.

The second picture is the communitarian one. This vision emphasizes individual rights less and solidarity more—among neighbors, workers, and citizens. Communitarians would discard liberal democracy as we know it and replace it with a more egalitarian, participatory society. They would abandon the market along with private ownership, so that individualism and self-interest would give way to a more social orientation.

Here is a case for the market solution. It is a more modest route but it has a better chance of succeeding. And it fosters libertarian values that, while not usually priorities for socialists, are nonetheless of great importance: individuality, privacy, freedom of choice, and opportunity to develop one's talents and abilities.

MARKET SOCIALISM

Market socialism initially gained a following in the 1920s within the social-democratic wing of Marxism. In the 1930s, Oskar Lange first laid out a full-fledged model. He saw a limited but critical role for central planning, to determine the rate of investment, for instance, and the distribution of income. The government would own all enterprises, and managers would aim to maximize profit. Many followers have since built on his vision, some favoring ownership by workers instead of citizens.

In a standard capitalist firm, individual owners or shareholders have the right to control the enterprise and take the profits. In market socialism, workers or citizens run the enterprise, appointing managers but retaining ultimate decision-making power either directly or through some representative body. Income accrues to the whole community of owners, to be distributed in a relatively egalitarian manner.

Market socialists tend to favor either public or worker ownership. But joint ownership or a mix of public and worker-owned businesses is also conceivable. Advocates of government ownership, on the one hand, argue that public firms tend to have greater access to capital and are more willing to take risks or pioneer new technology. Public distribution of income could ensure equality across society. Society would be acknowledging that enterprises are interdependent and would protect workers should their own enterprise do poorly, perhaps because of bad luck rather than merit.

On the other hand, worker ownership might provide stronger incentives to work hard and deliver high quality, since incomes would be tied to performance. The workplace might run more democratically, and workers might build greater solidarity through participation.

Clearly there are trade-offs in either case. A mixture of public and worker ownership would probably work best, including arrangements that sometimes separate the right to control the firm from the right to the income it generates.

TOM WEISSKOPF teaches economics at the University of Michigan and is co-author of *After the Wasteland: A Democratic Economics for the year 2000.*

> As long as capitalists are around, they will retain disproportionate power and continually challenge social democratic policies.

DOUG BEEKMAN

Public management would probably work best in industries with large economies of scale. It also makes sense for enterprises that generate important social costs and benefits: pollution, for instance, or innovations that have widespread application. Since income is easier to share than control, citizens and workers could each claim a share.

Even market socialists who favor worker ownership see a big role for government in regulating the market, far bigger than is usual under capitalism. Government would set a context for the market, making it serve social ends. Public bodies would steer clear of central planning, in the sense of deciding what quantities to produce and consume. Rather, government would focus on providing goods and services, on capital formation, and on taxes and subsidies. The difference between market socialism and capitalism in this respect is essentially one of degree rather than kind. Government would act much as it does in the more regulated, social-democratic capitalist systems.

DOUBTS

Skeptics of market socialism raise a number of challenges. Some argue that a market system is doomed to inefficiency and injustice, that it would continue to reward workers according to ability rather than effort and sacrifice. People would try to better themselves at the expense of oth-

ers, undermining the general interest. An elite group of "coordinators"—public investment bankers, managers, and planners—might gain the same kind of power that capitalists have enjoyed. Consumers and producers would act on selfish motives, competing instead of uniting. Society would encourage indifference rather than empathy. It's likely true that market socialism would breed a group of decision makers with more income and power than others. For markets to work, people do have to think of their own or their family's welfare first. Markets encourage anonymity, autonomy, and mobility.

But while inequality would persist, it would surely be much less than under capitalism, since market socialism eliminates income based on property ownership. Government could tax away unwarranted returns to workers based on their luck in the "generated lottery." There might still be differences based on skill, talent, position, and even chance, but disparities would pale by comparison to those that a propertied class creates. No complex economic system can assure anything close to full equality of income and power for everyone. There are bound to be differences in people's ability or desire to participate in decisions.

Anti-social behavior occurs in any society that permits some people to live better than others, and institutions that set limits are crucial. But after a point,

controls on selfish behavior can come only at the expense of privacy and freedom of choice. Market socialism does not directly foster community and empathy, yet it surely provides a friendlier environment for these values than capitalism does.

PREVENTION OR CURE

Market socialists share the same objectives as social democrats, but the groups have traditionally parted company on the best means to achieve their goals. While market socialism eliminates private ownership, social democracy constrains it. Lately, however, market socialists have moved closer to social democrats. While they still object to private ownership, they have come to support an expanding scope for markets. While most models of market socialism rule out stock markets, for instance, some theorists have suggested ways for non-owners to help finance enterprises and earn a share of the income without gaining any control over management. Most contemporary market-socialist models also allow for individual and small-scale private enterprise.

Market socialism and social democracy both see managers as profit-maximizers. And in either case, government would have to play a role in preventing managers from acting against the broader interests of society. One might well ask, then, why not go all the way? What compelling reason is there to rule out private ownership generally?

Eliminating private property certainly fosters greater equality of income. But government taxing and spending could conceivably do the same. Sweden's first three decades after World War II give the best example of social democracy at work. The government supported strong labor unions and highly redistributive taxing and spending. It acted to minimize unemployment while maintaining substantial labor mobility.

So why not simply provide a level playing field in which all types of businesses can compete? The answer is that market socialism is more secure. Tax-and-subsidy schemes and government regulation are much easier to reverse than changes in property rights. As long as capitalists are around, they retain disproportionate power and have a continuing interest in challenging social-democratic policies. Market socialism might well produce a kind of managerial class, but power would be spread more evenly because control of enterprise and income would be more dispersed.

PARTICIPATORY SOCIALISM

Though market socialism has become popular on the left in recent years, a much older tradition of participatory or communitarian socialism endures. Participatory socialists seek to revive Marx's original idea of a marketless society, free of the authoritarian rule and hierarchical, central planning that characterized the Communist-directed Soviet and Eastern European economies.

Among contemporary members of this school, Michael Albert and Robin Hahnel have worked out the most extensive model of how such an economy could operate. They advocate restructuring jobs to combine conceptual and manual work, so that conceptual workers would no longer dominate. People would rotate through a variety of positions, some more desirable than others. Society would distribute income according to need and effort, with each actor benefiting in proportion to the community as a whole. Everyone would have a say in deciding what to produce, by what method, and how to distribute it.

Worker councils in the workplace and consumer councils in the neighborhood would connect through a vast network. Worker councils would hook up to regional and industry council federations, and consumer councils would link to ward, city, county, state, and regional councils. A variety of boards would also help mesh all the small plans into a comprehensive one. Every single member of society, save the young and ill, would participate in councils. In place of prices, planners would rely on a system of accounting that measures and compares the social value of goods and services as well as the effort involved in producing them.

Advocates argue that such a system would promote democracy, equity, and solidarity without sacrificing efficiency. But the requirements for the system are so staggering as to invite skepticism. In addition to universal participation in councils and enormously sophisticated methods of measurement and accounting, the system would require some way for council and board members to work in a harmonious and timely fashion, and for the myriad plans developed at the ground level to be unified.

Even if such requirements could be met, one is bound to wonder whether it's worth it. Wouldn't participatory planning require so much time and energy that most people would get sick of it? Isn't participatory democracy so hard, time-consuming, and emotionally draining that it ought to be economized, used only for the most critical decisions?

COMMUNITY VS. LIBERTY

Participatory socialists reject the market not only for the way it allocates resources but also for the individualistic, competitive behavior it promotes. In place of the market, they suggest a number of other incentives. People could derive satisfaction from interesting work, or from fulfilling their responsibilities to others. Peer pressure and rules could discourage antisocial behavior, such as consuming too much or producing too little. But such a shift in incentives would surely require a wholesale conversion from *homo economicus* to what might be called *homo socialis*. Marxism teaches that the socio-economic environment strongly influences people, and that their values and behavior change as new economic systems evolve. So perhaps people can develop the attitudes to make a participatory system work. But it's not clear how we would make the transition.

Even if participatory socialism were feasible, there remain questions about whether it would be desirable. First of all, even without unusual wealth, some people might exercise more power because they were more interested in or better at using information or pressing their points of view.

Second, there is a danger that those holding minority views would be too vulnerable to the will of the majority. True democracy requires not only that people have more or less equal influence over decisions, but that those in the minority have protection or some escape from a decision that puts them at a disadvantage. In participatory socialism, recourse is limited. Every citizen has a voice in decisions, but if his or her view doesn't prevail, the opportunities for exit are limited. Changing jobs or neighborhoods remains possible, but it might be difficult.

In addition, there are drawbacks to rotating people through a variety of jobs. People may prefer to specialize, and some work requires considerable training and experience. Brain surgery and airplane piloting come to mind, as well as teaching, writing, and performing music

---

The case for market socialism is all too reasoned, too balanced, too moderate.

---

or sports.

Finally, the participatory system that Albert and Hahnel lay out would seem to threaten freedom of choice—how to live, what to consume, what kind of work to do, how to express oneself. People would have to justify many of their choices to some kind of collective body, which would surely set limits. A market system would provide much greater freedom. Of course, it does so only for people who can afford alternatives. That's why a market system that gives true freedom of choice must be reasonably free of income disparity.

The call for market socialism is not the kind of clarion call that brings political inspiration. The case is all too reasoned, too balanced, too moderate. This is its virtue, but also its Achilles heel. If it is to get anywhere, market socialism will need a strong political movement, and a political movement needs powerful rallying cries and popular mobilization. Market socialism needs to resonate more fully and clearly with public hopes and aspirations, or it will remain only a dream. ■

Real World Markets

Dollars & Sense, December 1986

White Lines, Bottom Lines

Profile of a mature industry

By Chris Tilly

The media recently have focused a great deal of attention on a small but rapidly growing industry, one dominated by a few foreign-based multinationals. This industry's sales in the United States have grown at an impressive rate, with shipments up by 325% between 1976 and 1984, despite U.S. government attempts to establish a strict quota on imports. Yearly retail sales in the business are estimated at $40 billion.

The industry's goods are particularly popular with the 18-to-25-year-old crowd: One person in six in this age group used them last year. However, the U.S. market for the products appears to be nearing saturation. U.S. market prices for the products have been falling since 1982. As a result, firms in the industry are trying out new products and searching for new markets.

CHRIS TILLY, a member of the *Dollars & Sense* Collective, teaches urban planning at the University of Lowell in Massachusetts.

The industry, in case you haven't guessed, is cocaine. Like any big business, the cocaine industry follows certain economic principles. A Miami attorney told the *Wall Street Journal,* "More than any other business I know, the drug business is pure capitalism, pure supply and demand."

SUCCESSFUL MULTINATIONAL

Most cocaine is grown from coca plants, then refined in Bolivia, Colombia, and Peru. These countries are economically dependent on the cocaine industry, one which Peru's President Alan Garcia calls Latin America's "only successful multinational." However, the bulk of the profits from the industry never reaches these countries.

The relationship of the Latin American supplier countries to the coca plant and its chemical derivatives could be called "supply-side dependency." Cocaine proceeds are estimated to account for one-quarter of Bolivia's gross national product, exceeding legal exports by $200 million or more. The cocaine industry employs as many as 100,000 Bolivians.

While Bolivia is an extreme case, Peru and Colombia are also "hooked." The drug trade brings $800 million annually into Peru—twice as much as copper exports. Colombia gains $600 million to $1 billion a year from cocaine exports.

That is not to say that these Latin American countries are getting rich. Cocaine follows a lengthy route from grower to consumer. Of the $75 street price of a gram of cocaine, about $60 goes to U.S. wholesalers and retailers. Only $2 per gram actually ends up in the hands of Latin American peasants and employees. Most of the remaining $13 earned by the Latin American cocaine entrepreneurs goes to foreign banks for laundering and safekeeping. One estimate is that Colombia's $1 billion in cocaine revenues is the result of trade worth $30 billion.

Meanwhile, these countries have experienced falling prices for other commodities, wiping out jobs. For example, Bolivia's revenues from tin and natural gas fell 70% in 1985 alone, and the Bolivian government has proposed sharply cutting back on employment in the tin mines.

At the base of the cocaine-production pyramid, the peasants and workers face few alternative sources of income. Even the $2 or less (per gram of cocaine) that peasants can earn represents much more than they can make otherwise. A peasant woman in the coca-growing region of Bolivia told the *New York Times* that her family earned ten times as much growing coca as they had earned with other crops. She added, "We couldn't live if it wasn't for the coca."

While U.S. crop-substitution programs offer Bolivian peasants $140 an acre to cultivate other crops, they can earn $2,000 to $4,000 an acre from coca. Sometimes U.S. trade and aid policies even spur drug production, as in Belize where cuts in U.S. sugar import quotas have turned a sugar-producing area into a marijuana-producing zone.

In addition to employment and earnings, a number of other threads tie Latin American countries to cocaine production. Foreigners' demand for pesos with which to buy cocaine keeps the value of the local currency up. When the Bolivian army launched its first raid into coca territory in 1984, the black market value of the peso dropped by two-thirds.

Cocaine serves political purposes, too. Producers use their wealth to win—or at least buy off—allies. With monthly salaries for police officers in Bolivia running as low as $25, buying complicity from the local police is not difficult. And some of the cocaine producers—such as reputed Colombian kingpin Pablo Escobar, who funded a slum redevelopment program—have won a reputation as "Robin Hoods." Finally, the *narcotraficantes* have their own armies, and can use the threat of assassination to pressure government officials.

ACROSS THE BORDER

According to the National Institute on Drug Abuse (NIDA, a division of the National Institutes of Health), over 20 million Americans have tried cocaine. But this fact alone does not constitute a "drug crisis."

Cocaine-related deaths, such as those of actor John Belushi and college basketball star Len Bias, have helped to propel cocaine into the headlines. But the 613 deaths due to cocaine last year pale in comparison to the 100,000 deaths due to alcohol (over 30 times the amount attributed to all illegal drugs taken together) and to the 350,000 deaths blamed on tobacco.

While cocaine use increased dramatically in the late 1970s, the percentage of the U.S. population who report using cocaine in the past year has remained roughly fixed since then. In fact, use of other illegal drugs is holding steady or declining, creating an overall *decline* in the rate of illicit drug use.

Cocaine is highly addictive. The National Narcotics Intelligence Consumers Commission estimated in 1981 that 6% of U.S. cocaine users consumed 60% of

the cocaine, using cocaine an average of 234 times a year. The demand for cocaine appears to be relatively inelastic—that is, cocaine use is unresponsive to changes in price. Heavy users would presumably pay almost anything to keep obtaining the drug.

Despite this inelastic demand, the street price of cocaine has been falling. Cocaine prices are currently almost 40% below their peak in 1982. All evidence points to a glut of cocaine on the U.S. market: supply has outrun demand. Cocaine has become a "mature industry."

In response, the cocaine industry has begun to diversify and expand. One of the new products is crack—cocaine in solid, smokable form. Arnold Washton, a psychopharmacologist at Fair Oaks Hospital in New Jersey, told *Newsweek*, "Crack itself is a marketing effort. Like fast food, it's a quick-sale product. [Because] it transforms the occasional user into an addictive user, it is much more likely to yield a repeat customer." Crack dealers are reaching out to a youth market, with prices of $10 to $15 per dose.

ENTER THE FEDS

In theory, government policies to reduce drug use could target either the supply- or demand-side of the cocaine market. So far, the Reagan administration's policies have focused primarily on the supply-side. But when demand is inelastic, decreasing the supply can be expected simply to drive prices up, attracting new suppliers into the market without significantly reducing the quantity consumed. Examination of the results of three supply-side policies—interdiction, eradication, and enforcement—confirms this expectation.

Interdiction—stopping drugs at a country's borders—has been somewhat effective at stopping marijuana imports, resulting in a shift to domestic cultivation of cannabis. A second result of interdiction efforts has been to lead smugglers to switch their operations from marijuana to cocaine, a substance which is less bulky, easier to conceal, and which brings a much higher price per ounce with little difference in the legal penalties for getting caught. A third outcome of the federal government's focus on interdiction has led cocaine importers in south Florida to move to supply routes across the Mexican border. The federal Drug Enforcement Agency claims that interdiction captures about a quarter of the cocaine entering the United States, but this figure is probably inflated.

Eradication involves ending the cultivation and refinement of drugs in their source countries. Again, there is a "success" story: During the 1970s, under U.S. pressure, Mexico wiped out much of its marijuana and heroin crops. But as a result, Colombia simply took Mexico's place in the marijuana business, and opened up the cocaine market to Colombian producers as well.

The recent raids on Bolivian cocaine refineries by Bolivian and U.S. troops have been fiascos. Understandably, not everyone in the Bolivian government and the armed forces supported the elimination of Bolivia's major export, and leaks

get caught) are easily replaced. The most likely consequence of stepped-up enforcement is increased repression in poor communities, without much decrease in the flow of drugs.

What about government intervention on the demand side? Two key elements of a strategy to cut demand for cocaine would have to be drug treatment programs (to help heavy users) and preventive education. The Reagan administra-

But between supply-side dependency and inelastic demand, this strategy is unlikely to reduce drug use.

UP IN SMOKE

The NIDA claims that a larger proportion of young people use illegal drugs in the United States than in any other industrialized country. Why do so many people turn to illegal drugs? Certainly part of the reason is that our culture condones and even glorifies the use of other (legal) addictive substances such as alcohol, nicotine, and caffeine.

All evidence points to a glut of cocaine on the U.S. market: Supply has outrun demand. Cocaine has become a "mature industry."

---

allowed drug producers to clear out before the strike forces arrived. One effect of the raids has been to establish a precedent for intervention by U.S. armed forces, and many Bolivians are angered by them. When over 100 Bolivian and American drug agents raided the town of Santa Ana in October 1985, 3,000 of the town's 5,000 people rushed to the town square, rallied by the ringing of church bells. Shouting "Kill the Yankees," they surrounded the agents and chased them out of town.

Even if the cocaine business were driven out of Bolivia, Colombia, and Peru, there are plenty of other poor Latin American and Caribbean countries that would be hard put to refuse the dollars that the industry brings. Already, coca cultivation is spreading to Brazil, Ecuador, and Venezuela.

A final supply-side strategy is law enforcement—jailing drug dealers. Despite the clamor made by the President and Congress about imposing harsh sentences and even the death penalty for dealers, this strategy is unlikely to make much of a dent in the cocaine trade. Overworked police departments, clogged courts, and overcrowded prisons simply can't accommodate large numbers of dealers—except by letting other crimes go. And street-level dealers (the ones who

tion has substantially cut funding for both. The Department of Education's drug education budget fell from $14 million in 1981 to less than $3 million in 1985. Reagan has proposed allotting an additional $100 million for drug treatment programs, but advocates for these programs point out that this "addition" would only bring their funding back up to 1980 levels.

Instead of these programs, the administration has made "voluntary" drug testing and Nancy Reagan's "Just Say No" clubs the real center pieces of its demand-side strategy. The clubs have about 200,000 high school age members, but nobody knows just how many of them are actually saying "no" outside the club meetings.

The drug tests introduce a new level of surveillance without much promise of eliminating drug use. Inexpensive versions of the urine test have a 20% rate of "false positives"—test results that falsely show drug use. And without access to treatment programs, people "caught" using cocaine may be more likely to lose their jobs than to quit the drug.

In short, the Reagan administration's strategy for the "war on drugs" is more repression: repression in the producer countries of Latin America, on the borders, in the streets, and in the workplaces.

Another reason is that drugs are a distraction from the tedium and alienation of jobs, schools, and living environments. "I don't know if you've had the opportunity to stand in a pit and turn a screwdriver over your head hour after hour, but I have," Dr. Douglas Talbott, president of the American Academy of Additionology, commented to *Newsweek*. "It's almost like torture. These people bring mind-altering drugs to ease the boredom, the tension, and the stress of doing their job." Dr. Wesley Westman, head of the alcohol and drug dependency center at the Miami Veterans Administration hospital was quoted in *Time* as saying, "Cocaine is the drug of choice by people who are into the American dream—'I love my job, I am successful'—except that they don't and they're not." And in the inner city, especially among low-income people of color, the widespread use of crack means that the drug has evolved into much more than a suburbanite fix: It is helping to destroy the social fabric of these communities.

But the leaders of the crusade against illegal drug use seem oblivious to these issues. Like the U.S. government's "war on poverty," the "war on drugs" is a determined assault on a set of symptoms, combined with an equally determined disregard for its underlying causes. ■

Dollars & Sense, September 1990

Aborting Choice

Abortion restrictions hurt poor women most

By Randy Albelda

In the wake of a growing number of restrictions on abortion services around the country, a woman's ability to get an abortion increasingly depends on how much money she has and where she lives. Women with money or access to money will continue to be able to get abortions, while poor women will suffer the most from recent assaults on abortion rights.

Since last year's *Webster v. Reproductive Health Services* Supreme Court decision, several states have passed laws restricting abortion services. As the supply of abortion services diminishes, the demand for abortions will remain strong, and the price of abortions will rise. Like all market transactions, the effects of price increases are not neutral. Having lost most federal funding of abortions several years ago, poor women will be hurt the most while all women will be forced to pay more.

WHO GETS ABORTIONS

Close to two-thirds of all women have at least one unintended pregnancy in their lives, according to a report on abortion and women's health by the Alan Guttmacher Institute, a private, non-profit organization that researches family planning. Of women who get pregnant unintentionally, close to half terminate their pregnancy by abortion, 13% have miscarriages, and 40% have their babies.

In a 1987 survey, the most common reason for having an abortion (76% of respondents) was that the woman was not ready for how a baby would change her life—specifically, a baby would interfere with employment, school, or other responsibilities. About 68% said they could not afford a baby because they were single, unemployed, or a student. Just over half the sample said they were seeking an abortion because they did not want to raise a child alone.

Women who have abortions are more likely to be young, poor, non-white, and unmarried than the average of all women of child-bearing age. About 60% of all women who get abortions are under the age of 25. One-third of all women who have abortions have family incomes below $11,000, while in the population as a whole, 15% of all women between 15 and 44 years of age live in families with incomes below that amount. Fewer than one out of every five women getting an abortion is married, despite the fact that almost one out of every two women of child-bearing age is married. Compared to other women, black women and Latinas are more likely to get abortions, while Catholics are more likely to have an abortion than are Jewish or Protestant women.

LEGAL PATCHWORK

Since the 1989 *Webster* ruling, an uneven pattern of abortion statutes across the states has emerged, similar to the patchwork of laws that existed during the eight years prior to the 1973 *Roe v. Wade* decision legalizing abortion. As states impose more restrictions, a woman's access to legal abortions will depend on where she lives and how much money she has.

The *Webster* decision upheld a Missouri law that was among the most restrictive in the nation, opening the way for other states to curb abortion services. Since then, several states have approved laws obstructing abortion services, ranging from parental consent laws to stricter stipulations on who can provide abortions. These developments increase the cost of abortions, either directly through changing where a woman can get an abortion or indirectly through limiting the supply of abortions.

Many of the new laws hurt low-income women the most. The Missouri statute bans abortions in public hospitals (even if no public funds are used) and prohibits public employees from participating in abortions except to save a woman's life. Only 13% of all abortions were performed in hospitals around the country in 1985. However, low-income women and women of color are much more likely to have their abortions in a hospital than white middle-class women.

At the same time, several states have enacted requirements that abortions, especially in the second trimester, be performed in hospitals instead of outpatient clinics. Because a hospital abortion typically costs two to three times as much as a clinic abortion, this mandate once again hits poor women the hardest.

Faced with higher-priced abortions and a lack of public funding, poor women need more time to raise the necessary

RANDY ALBELDA, a member of the *Dollars & Sense* Collective, teaches economics at the University of Massachusetts at Boston.

Close to two-thirds of all women have at least one unintended pregnancy in their lives.

The ultimate cost of limiting the supply of abortions is death.

funds. Delaying the procedure until later in the pregnancy increases both the costs and the health risks. Abortions performed in the eleventh or twelfth week of pregnancy are three times more dangerous than abortions performed in the eighth week, and the risks increase as the pregnancy progresses. The average fee for an abortion performed in a clinic within the first 12 weeks of pregnancy was $247 last year, while the average price soared to $697 for an abortion at 20 weeks of pregnancy.

In addition to price increases for the abortion procedure itself, women will have to pick up other costs of limited access to abortion services. Women who cannot get an abortion near their homes will also have to pay transportation and possibly accommodation costs.

THE BUCK STOPS HERE

Few women are able to turn to public funding to cover these increased costs. Congress has restricted or prohibited the use of federal Medicaid funds for abortions since 1976, when the Hyde Amendment was passed. Federal funds are currently available for abortions only when the life of the woman is endangered by pregnancy. The federal government paid for just 322 abortions in 1987, and that included some services following miscarriages. Only 13 states use their own revenues to provide medically necessary abortions for low-income women, the Guttmacher Institute reported earlier this year.

Of women who would obtain a publicly funded abortion if they could, up to 80% raise the money to pay for an abortion themselves. To pay for the procedure, many buy less food or clothing or let other bills go unpaid; a majority report that the abortion was a serious financial hardship. A small percentage of women who are unable to get public funding attempt self-induced abortions, or seek an abortion from an unregulated, illegal provider.

The ultimate cost of limiting the supply of abortions is death. A conservative estimate of the number of deaths attributed to abortions was 193 in 1965, when abortion was illegal in every state except when the pregnancy threatened the mother's life. Over half of these deaths were women of color. The number of deaths declined after 1970, when 15 states liberalized abortion laws, and continued to fall after the 1973 Roe v. Wade decision. In 1985, from the 1.6 million legal abortions performed, six women are known to have died.

UNWANTED CHILDREN

Restrictions on the supply of abortion services, combined with earlier bans on public funding, will cause more women to bear more unwanted children and to struggle with the accompanying financial costs. As a result of public funding bans in the late 1970s, 20% of women who would have received a Medicaid-funded abortion in 1980 carried their unwanted pregnancy to term.

In purely economic terms, being a mother involves heavy financial burdens. Besides the obvious costs attached to rearing children (such as adequate health care, clothing, and food), a major cost is lost wages. Because women still do most child care, they must often quit a job or school to care for young children.

Women who leave the labor force temporarily or interrupt their education also lose work experience and skills. Women with discontinuous work experience obtain smaller salary bases and fewer raises than workers who never left the labor force. And although schooling for women does not pay off as much as for men, women with more education make more than women with less education.

Women who must work while also caring for children, including many single mothers, face additional constraints. First, child-care responsibilities reduce the time available to work. Second, women on the average earn less than men. The combination of limited time and low wages can be devastating, as is suggested by the fact that poverty rates for single mothers are six times that of married couples.

Even if every state outlawed abortions, women would still have them. Limiting abortion services will never eliminate the demand for these services. Only by reducing the number of unintended pregnancies and the cost of having children will there be less demand for abortions.

Women in the United States have a higher rate of unintended pregnancies than women in Canada and almost all Western European countries, despite similar birthrates. Compared to these countries, the United States has a relatively low use of contraceptives. It's no wonder U.S. women are more likely to seek an abortion than their European and Canadian sisters. Safer contraceptive devices and increased educational services would help reduce the demand for abortions.

But while birth control reduces the likelihood of pregnancy, it does not eliminate it. In 1987, 43% of all women with unintended pregnancies were using some form of birth control. More widespread use of contraceptives will not eliminate unintended pregnancies.

Neither recent developments in the battle over abortion nor the tactics of abortion opponents have eliminated women's need for safe, cheap abortions. While abortion opponents want to restrict the supply of abortions, they also condemn birth control and fail to promote policies that would reduce the demand for abortions by easing the financial burden of parenting. As long as women need abortions, limiting the supply of abortions penalizes women in general, and poor women the most. ■

RESOURCES: The Alan Guttmacher Institute, *Abortion and Women's Health: A Turning Point for America?*, 1990; Rachel Benson Gold and Sandra Guardado, "Public Funding of Family Planning, Sterilization and Abortion Services, 1987," *Family Planning Perspectives*, September/October 1988.

Dollars & Sense, January 1986

A Real Look at Rent Control

Before Santa Monica voted for rent control in April 1979, the anti-rent control forces distributed a postcard bearing a photograph of an abandoned five-story brick tenement, its ground floor windows boarded up. On the back a printed message warned: "This is a New York City apartment building, devastated by rent control. Don't let it happen here!"

The charge is not a new one. Scenes of burnt-out buildings in the South Bronx are invariably linked with the grim specter of rent control. Shortages of new apartments and the decay or abandonment of old ones have also been attributed to these legal constraints on landlords' profits.

In 1982, tenant groups were fighting in all major U.S. cities and in many suburbs to save affordable rental housing from extinction. Yet rent control as a strategy remains plagued by its bad reputation—a reputation it doesn't deserve. Cities with rent control may have problems with housing abandonment and decay, but so do their non-rent-controlled counterparts. There is no evidence that rent control leads to lower rates of construction or less maintenance. In fact, none of the apartments shown in the Santa Monica postcard were subject to rent control at the time the building was abandoned.

On the other hand, rent control by itself is not a solution to housing problems. Many renters suffer as much from low incomes as from high rents. Even a strict rent control law would not ensure adequate affordable housing.

THE NITTY GRITTY

Rent control has been around since the early 1900s and was an integral part of the socialist movement in the United States by 1920. Rents were frozen nationwide during World War II, and New York City enacted its own rent control law immediately after the wartime freeze was lifted. But for most of the next two decades, no other cities had rent control.

In the early 1970s, the growth of the civil rights and student movements combined with inflation to create a push for rent control laws. New Jersey, California, and Massachusetts enacted "local option" laws, which permitted individual municipalities to pass rent control laws. During the same period, other cities tried to enact rent control laws which were either voted down (as in Ann Arbor and East Lansing) or declared unconstitutional (Miami Beach). By the latter part of the 1970s, rent control movements had lost momentum; the passage of rent control in Santa Monica represented a rare victory in that period.

Today about 100 communities have some form of rent control. While they are not all large cities (Bayonne, New Jersey, for example), almost without exception they are concentrated on the East and West Coasts, where rental units make up an important part of the housing market.

Most of these cities have what is called *moderate* rent control. These laws allow rents to increase if operating costs (such as the price of fuel) and maintenance costs rise. Some cities also allow rents to rise by the rate of inflation each year. In cities where landlords are only permitted to pass on cost increases, rents tend to rise more slowly, since typically only half the rent money collected goes to operating costs. (The rest goes to paying off the mortgage and to profits.)

In addition, most moderate rent control laws exempt new construction from rent control, either initially or permanently. Many cities also now have vacancy decontrol, which permits a onetime rent increase when tenants move or are evicted.

Some communities have *loose* rent control (also know as "market-based" or "fair rate of return" laws). These statutes generally peg rents to the levels charged in nearby cities without rent control, and exert little control over the rent level. While loose rent control may protect renters in neighborhoods experiencing rapid speculative rent increases, it is of little use in maintaining affordable housing for the community as a whole.

Restrictive rent control laws, such as those which existed in New York City until 1970, would actually freeze rents for all tenants, or at least for poor tenants. Recent attempts to enact restrictive laws have been struck down in court as unconstitutional—as violating landlords' rights to a "fair rate of return" and to protection from "unreasonable seizure" of property. No city currently has restrictive rent control.

Opponents of rent control argue that such laws make it unprofitable to maintain, build, or own multifamily housing. However, an examination of current rent control laws and their impact on city housing casts doubt on this argument. In a city where the rents are adjusted by the rate of inflation each year, a landlord will always receive the same net profit as s/he

Cities with rent control may have problems with housing abandonment and decay, but so do their non-rent controlled counterparts.

earned at the time of the law's enactment. In addition, the landlord will benefit from any increase in the value of his or her building. The rent control law itself will not cut into landlords' profits and drive landlords out of business.

A comparison of rent-controlled cities with similar cities without rent control further contradicts the grim picture painted by opponents. To start, it is often alleged that rent control discourages new construction. Opponents point to the case of New Jersey, where many cities enacted some form of rent control during 1973 or 1974. In these cities, apartment construction fell by 52% between the periods 1970-72 (pre-rent control) and 1975-77. However, apartment construction in New Jersey cities without rent control dropped by 88% over the same period. The housing problem has been felt nationwide, indicating broad structural causes beyond local constraints on landlord profits.

The most serious charge against rent control is that it leads to housing decay and abandonment. Abandonment occurs when landlords stop maintaining and paying taxes on a building. As the building falls into serious disrepair, tenants gradually abandon the decaying structure. Rent control, however, is at most a minor contributing factor to housing abandonment. A 1978 housing study done by the federal government showed that eight cities reported major abandonment problems (Camden, Cleveland, Gary, Lynn, New York City, Oakland, St. Louis, and Toledo). Out of these, only New York City had some form of rent control.

More detailed studies of abandonment in New York City have reached the same conclusion. In Manhattan, neighborhoods where a high proportion of apartments are rent-controlled typically have little abandonment. Even in the South Bronx, rent control seems not to have been the major cause of abandonment. In 1977, the Women's City Club, one of the oldest civic organizations in New York City, made a very detailed examination of 38 individual buildings in a neighborhood undergoing abandonment in the South Bronx. Based on data from a five-year period, they concluded that the chances of a building becoming abandoned were not related to the maxi-

Rent control and profits

What is the effect of rent control on landlord profits? The total profit from owning an apartment building comes from three sources: operating profits, tax write-offs, and increases in the value of the building (capital gains). Operating profits are the difference between the rents that a landlord collects and her/his costs—primarily mortgage payments and the costs of fuel and maintenance.

Owning an apartment building also allows the landlord to pay less taxes on other income. The tax laws include the fiction that a building depreciates each year (even when its value is going up). The amount of depreciation can be deducted from the landlord's other income, lowering total taxes.

The third type of profit is capital gains. Buildings can increase in value either because of inflation, or because of a sudden upsurge of housing demand in a neighborhood. The second type of capital gains is always profit. Gains from inflation may or may not be profitable for the landlord, depending on when the building was bought. If the building was bought before

the inflation of the 1970s, then the mortgage is either paid off or has a very low interest rate. In this case, any gains from inflation represent pure profit. For more recent mortgages, the banks anticipated inflation and charged higher interest rates (so that effectively, mortgage payments rise with inflation).

What rent control does is take away the chance for landlords to earn big profits from capital gains. Without rent control, when a neighborhood suddenly becomes upgraded the landlord can either boost rents sharply or sell out and make big bucks. With rent control, rent increases are limited so the value of the building does not soar. But moderate rent control does not eliminate operating profits or the tax advantages from owning an apartment building.

In effect, rent control limits landlords to a normal rate of profit and keeps them from collecting big windfalls. It may also sometimes squeeze small landlords more than big ones, but on average it should not eliminate profits for anyone.

mum level of rent permitted in that building. They found that abandonment more often resulted from depressed renter incomes and high interest rates faced by landlords.

There is also no evidence that rent control even reduces the level of maintenance of a building. Separate studies of maintenance expenditures in Massachusetts and New Jersey found little difference in spending levels between similar rent-controlled and nonrent-controlled buildings.

Because moderate rent control may reduce but does not eliminate landlord profits, the current laws have minimal negative effects. On the other hand, most cities with rent control now also have a very high demand for housing. In the

absence of rent control, rent increases in these cities would likely have far exceeded the rate of inflation.

Under these conditions, rent control can afford some protection to middle- and lower-income tenants, keeping a mix of people in gentrifying areas. Moreover, limiting residential rent increases may also provide some protection for small businesses and light industry. Regulation of apartment rents may prevent the switching of land and buildings to residential uses—a tactic which becomes highly profitable when gentrification occurs.

The benefits from rent control are not evenly distributed among all groups of tenants, however. Since many cities have vacancy decontrol, the elderly and long-term stable households benefit from the low levels of their original rent. People just entering the rental market and renters who move frequently tend to pay higher rents.

Moreover, rent control cannot prevent low-priced apartments from being abandoned, renovated, or converted to condominiums. Nor can it stop the trend toward the construction of high-priced luxury apartments. Rent control holds down the rents for individual apartments. But the replacement of low-priced apartments with luxury models may still cause the average rent in a city to rise rapidly.

A HELPFUL HINT

The shortage of affordable rental units is not just restricted to a few large cities—it is a national problem. Between 1970 and 1983, the median share of income going to rent rose from 20% to 30%. This was not a small change. Since the 1880s, the rule of thumb has been "a week's wage for a month's rent." This 25% standard in fact reflected actual conditions for most of this century, with poor tenants paying more and wealthier tenants paying less of their incomes in rent. The shift to 30% conceals a much larger change for poor tenants. In 1980 renters with incomes under $3,000 paid more than 72% of their income in rent, while those with incomes between $3,000 and $7,000 paid 47% of their income.

However, rent control would not have solved this problem. Surprisingly, overall rent levels did not rise much during the 1970s. In 1970 the median rent was $108; in 1983 it was $315. Adjusted for inflation, median rents rose only by 14% over the last 15 years. In addition, most of this increase reflected the abandonment of low-priced apartments and their replacement by high-priced apartments. Rents on individual apartments actually rose, on average, slower than the rate of inflation in all large metropolitan areas through the 1970s and early 1980s.

Meanwhile, the primary cause of the housing affordability problem was the increasing poverty of tenants. During the 1970s, homeownership was very attractive and many who could afford to do so bought a home. The result was that the composition of tenant households changed. Between 1970 and 1980, fami-

lies headed by married couples dropped from 54% to 35% of the renting population. The remaining renters were more likely to be single-parent households with lower incomes. As a result, the median income of renters, adjusted for inflation, dropped by 25% between 1970 and 1983, while the real income of homeowners only decreased by 2%.

If moderate rent control had been enacted nationwide during the 1970s, it would have kept some but not most rents down. Moreover, it would not have touched the main affordability problem—the increasing mismatch between high-priced luxury apartments being built and low-income families looking for rental shelter. It could not therefore have completely prevented the drastic increase in the percentage of renter income paid for housing.

RENT CONTROL IN THE 1980S

According to Peter Marcuse, a housing activist who teaches urban planning at Columbia University, rents will rise much faster in the 1980s. Throughout the 1970s, the value of apartment buildings was increasing rapidly from inflation, providing large capital gains to landlords. This combined with the shift from renting to homeownership to lessen upward pressures on rents.

In the 1980s, however, inflation has slowed, decreasing the capital gains accruing to landlords. Moreover, stagnant

incomes and the high cost of buying a home have produced a new group of middle-class "permanent renters"—people who would have bought a home in the past but who can't afford one now. Landlords are now in a good position to demand higher rents.

As a result, the pressure for some form of rent control is increasing, creating the possibility of new coalitions between low- and middle-income tenants (although historically such coalitions have tended to submerge the goals of lower-income tenants to those of other members). Peter Marcuse expects rent control to be a likely strategy for such a coalition. He suggests that direct action, like rent strikes or squatting, involves high personal risks and can expose tenants to direct landlord or police pressure. At the other extreme, campaigns for increased public subsidies are often too remote in their targets and too diffuse in their impact to generate major mass involvement. Rent control is local and direct, and the issues are familiar to everyone, making it an easier goal for emerging coalitions.

Rent control by itself is not a complete housing policy, however. An effective housing policy would include provisions for rent subsidies and public housing. Rent control is but one step toward moving housing allocation from the market to the public domain. ∎

Dollars & Sense, November 1988

Endangered Species

The uncertain future of low-income housing

By Lynn Shields

Low-rent housing is harder than ever to find and to hang on to. The Reagan years have capped a decade and a half of increasing hardship for low-income renters, decimating the supply of affordable housing. The result is a shelter crisis the likes of which this country hasn't witnessed since the Great Depression.

The worst is yet to come. By most projections, the long-term inability of the private sector to meet low-income housing needs, coupled with slashed federal housing programs in the 1980s portends a future shock in affordable housing. Homelessness in the 1980s could be the calm before the storm.

The supply of low-rent housing has never been adequate, but people with limited means are increasingly trapped in a tightening squeeze between falling real incomes and soaring rents. Between 1970 and 1983, rents rose twice as fast as incomes. By 1986, the real median income of all renters had fallen 10% from its 1972 level.

That combination means that adequate housing is out of reach for more and more low-income households. The traditional rule of thumb allotted 25% of income to shelter costs. By 1983, 83% of households earning less than $10,000

LYNN SHIELDS is a doctoral candidate in urban planning at the Massachusetts Institute of Technology.

were paying more than this, up from 48% of those earning the same real income in 1970.

Federal housing programs, primary targets of Reagan's henchmen, once offered some reprieve, but no longer. When Reagan took office, the military got seven dollars for every federal dollar spent on housing. As the end of his tenure approaches, that ratio will be 44 to 1. Exacerbating the cuts in public-sector housing programs, the current administration implemented tax and banking policies that discourage the private sector from providing low-rent housing.

The result is unprecedented demand for the low-rent housing that does exist. Vacancy rates for low-rent apartments have fallen to 1% or 2% in major cities; in Boston, the rate is effectively zero.

THE PRIVATE SLIDE

The anchor of conservative ideology, the private market, has failed miserably in recent years to provide shelter for the poor. While the shortage of affordable housing is not new, as recently as the mid-1970s the situation appeared less desperate. The trickle-down process provided a little help: as some housing built for the middle class deteriorated, it became more affordable. In addition, attractive financing for construction and rehabilitation, plus generous tax breaks, fostered the production of multi-family housing that could be made available to low-income households. As of 1974, almost 11 million private units rented for

$250 per month or less. Assuming that 30% of household income would be devoted to housing, about 9 million households needed those homes.

Nevertheless, the aggregate numbers obscured a more depressing reality. For example, the 1974 figures do not reflect severe shortages in low-rent housing that existed in some regions of the country. And poorly enforced or non-existent housing codes meant that a great deal of low-rent housing was unfit to live in. Finally, low-income people occupied only a portion of these units: they had to compete with others in the private market, including middle-income Americans who didn't own homes.

By the halfway point of the Reagan reign, the lack of affordable housing had become obvious by any measure. That lack was, as Jonathan Kozol illustrates in *Rachel's Children,* a direct cause of the homelessness that is a visible national shame. In 1983, 12 million households needed low-rent apartments, but the supply had dropped below 9 million. The 25% yardstick was forgotten—as Kozol points out, six million U.S. renters now pay more than half their household income for housing.

The widening gap between need and the private supply has several causes. On one end, overall rents are rising rapidly, led by those in San Francisco, New York, and Boston. In 1986, only 7.5% of the private sector's new, multi-family dwellings rented for less than $300 per month. In Boston, 80% of the units that rented for under $300 in 1982 couldn't be had for that price in 1984, but over the same period the number of units renting for over $600 more than doubled.

While costs rise, the supply shrinks. Some unfit housing has met a well deserved end by demolition, while other units have been transformed into condos. Kozol cites a 1984 National Housing Law Project estimate that 500,000 low-income units are being lost annually to condo and coop conversions, abandonment, arson, and demolition. Another traditional source of low-income housing, single-room occupancy boarding houses and hotels, has also been lost, in this case to gentrification as central-city living returned to fashion.

In the years to come, the chasm between housing needs and private-sector housing costs will likely deepen. One reason is the 1986 tax reform, which could dampen investment in low-income housing. U.S. tax policy had provided de facto incentives to increase the shelter supply—for example, by making investments in housing more attractive. Even though the middle class and the rich occupied most new housing, the trickle-down effect relieved some pressure on the low-income supply.

That barely helped, but the 1986 reform might make matters worse. By reducing deductions for interest and real-estate taxes and slowing depreciation deductions, it could discourage real estate investment. Similarly, the reform eliminates favorable tax rates for capital gains, and it restricts the power of states to issue tax-exempt bonds, which had been a source of below-market interest rates for financing housing. While some of these tax changes could have a progressive element, they should have been accompanied by policies that explicitly encourage affordable housing.

Changes in the investment climate could also shrink the housing supply and shift the focus toward high-income rental projects and condos, both of which are more apt to yield fast profits. Savings and loan institutions—known as thrifts— have been a major source of residential lending for the middle class. They also were significant investors in smaller multi-family buildings.

As long as the thrifts paid low interest rates to depositors, they could use the deposits to write low-interest-rate mortgages. However, these institutions are playing a diminishing role in financing housing. Deregulation and rising interest rates have taken their toll—a quarter of thrifts have disappeared since the mid-1970s, and one in five of those remaining is in trouble. Nor are the survivors a source of bargain mortgages: They have lost their supply of cheap money, since they must now offer competitive interest on deposits.

Taking such changes into account, MIT city planner Phillip Clay anticipates that the private sector's limited role in low-rent housing will shrink even more. In a study for the Neighborhood Reinvestment Corp. of Washington, D.C., he estimates that "there will be some shrinking in the stock of unsubsidized low-rent units—at least 20% and perhaps more—if the worst fears of tax reform and more conservative urban lending come to fruition."

PUBLIC PULLBACK

Conventional economic wisdom says that when a commodity is in short supply, prices will rise, stimulating additional production. That view only considers people with the money to buy the commodity, leaving out low-income housing, since millions of Americans are unable to pay the requisite price.

For a half-century, the public sector has responded to this gap to some extent with a variety of low-rent housing programs. Federally assisted endeavors—public housing, tenant rent subsidies, and subsidies to providers of low-income housing—currently account for more than four million units.

As with the private stock, public-sector housing programs are in jeopardy, making them a weak hope for meeting future affordable housing needs. Only one in five eligible households currently benefits from some form of federally subsidized housing. In the future, that assistance will be available to even fewer low-income families.

Housing owned by the federal government and administered by local housing authorities is the largest single program serving the shelter needs of low-income people. Begun as a New Deal project in 1937, the public housing system included approximately 1.35 million units in 1985. Even that large number did not come close to satisfying demand. A 1986 survey of the largest public housing authorities indicated they had waiting lists equal to or exceeding the total number of public units in each locality. It is becoming increasingly common for families to double up while they await housing. Clearly, the situation is going from bad to unbearable.

Modernization is also taking a toll on public housing. As the bonds that financed public housing construction are paid off, local housing authorities are free to offer units to higher-income tenants. Since affordable housing is in short supply even for the middle class, this will further decrease the supply of housing for low-income families. For example, Boston's Columbia Point project is being converted to mixed-income use, eliminating two-thirds of the low-income units.

Moreover, at least some public housing units will be lost to the private sector. In 1985, the Department of Housing and Urban Development (HUD) proposed a demonstration program to sell its public housing to tenants. Although the project

covers only 2,000 units, the implications are great if the project is implemented on a wide scale. Housing activists see the sale partly as a way for the federal government to abdicate its responsibility to house the poor. And the agency has no intention of building new units, despite the continuing intense shortage.

Perhaps most critical is the imminent expiration of federal programs that encourage the private sector to provide low-rent housing. As of 1985, 1.9 million privately owned low-rent units received federal subsidies for construction or operating costs. Federal mortgage insur-

UPPING THE ANTE

Looking to the future, Clay has made grim predictions about the total supply of affordable housing. His conclusions are frightening for the millions of low-income Americans who rely on government programs to solve their shelter crisis. Adding together private and public units, he calculates that between 1983 and 2003, 3.5 million low-rent units—27% of the supply of subsidized housing—will be lost. But 5.3 million more households—an increase of 49%—will need low-rent housing.

ing increasingly necessary. Thus, the program would replace the profit incentive with social goals as the guide for the supply, cost, quality, location, and use of housing.

The program contains three components to reduce housing costs. One piece would eliminate debt as a housing cost for consumers, in part by substituting capital grants for loans in financing new and rehabilitated units. On existing units, outstanding debt would be retired in a similar way. Second, low-income families would receive a housing allowance, analogous to Section 8 subsidies. Third, much of existing housing would move into the public sector. Homeowners faced with foreclosure could voluntarily transfer their property to the public sector, giving up ownership in exchange for lifetime tenure and rent subsidies. Involuntary transfers of rental housing would be made if the landlord is delinquent in taxes or mortgage payments or violates housing codes.

The program would be federally mandated but locally administered, tying federal funding to compliance with the principles of the program. The price tag, estimated at $5 billion annually for the next decade, roughly equals the current loss to the federal budget of tax deductions for homeowners.

Congress is considering two pieces of legislation supporting the social housing program. Rep. Ronald Dellums (D-Calif.) has proposed one version, with slightly different budget amounts. A bill introduced by Rep. Barney Frank (D-Mass.) has a more limited budget and is less far-reaching in applying the principle of social ownership or housing.

This legislation has little chance to pass soon, but as Chester Hartman, one of the study's authors, states, "It raises the ante and calls for fundamental change in the housing system." Indeed, to meet the need, change is required—soon. ∎

The proposal's core is the concept of home ownership: Housing would be operated for residential and community benefit and not sold for profit.

ance, for example, guarantees payment by the government if the developer defaults. This provides financing that otherwise would not be available, but only under the condition that a certain number of units be occupied by low-income tenants. Operating cost subsidies are available for specific units that must be occupied by income-eligible tenants. In each of these cases, the contracts that limit the units to low-income tenants have termination dates, which vary from program to program. If alternative means of maintaining these as affordable units aren't found, then the units could be lost permanently from the low-rent market when their contracts and use restrictions expire.

Not only is the existing stock of subsidized housing disappearing, but new subsidized units are being supplied more slowly. From 1976 to 1982, more than one million new, federally subsidized units augmented the supply of private low-rent housing. Since then, fewer than 25,000 units have been produced annually, not enough to replace those lost to sales or old age.

The potential loss of affordable housing is alarming. If unchecked, the human costs will be substantial. Undoubtedly, these costs will be borne by those with the fewest financial resources—women, minorities, and children. Summing up the situation, one tenant states, "It's not the American dream."

Working under the auspices of the Institute for Policy Studies, a national task force has crafted a comprehensive alternative, a program whose basic principle asserts that "every person is entitled to adequate housing in a decent neighborhood at an affordable price." The task force took particular notice of "the special housing needs of women, minorities and others traditionally disadvantaged in the housing market."

The proposal's core is the concept of social ownership: housing would be operated for residential and community benefit and not sold for profit. This concept is designed to address what the authors cite as the underlying cause of the crisis—treating housing as a commodity. With the federal government abandoning its housing role, such an approach is becom-

RESOURCES: Jonathan Kozol, *Rachel's Children*; Phillip L. Clay, "At Risk of Loss: The Endangered Future of Low-Income Rental Housing Resources," Neighborhood Reinvestment Corporation, May 1987; "A Decent Place To Live: The Report of the National Housing Task Force," March 1988.

Consumers

Dollars & Sense, December 1990

Saturday Morning Pushers

Toy industry takes over kids' television

By Nancy Carlsson-Paige & Diane E. Levin

Trying to please their children, parents all over the country face tremendous pressure to buy the latest and hottest toys. Many parents—and aunts, uncles, and grandparents—bemoan the limited choices toy stores present. The market offers little more than violence for boys and passivity for girls.

Who's Calling the Shots? How to Respond Effectively to Children's Fascination with War Play and War Toys describes the ways in which today's war toys are more destructive than those used by earlier generations. Authors **Nancy Carlsson-Paige** and

Diane E. Levin argue that toys designed for one specific use impose a script on children's play and discourage more creative development. The authors offer practical ideas to help children and parents reclaim control over play, combat consumerism and sex-role stereotyping, and find alternatives to violence.

In the following adaptation from the book, **Dollars & Sense** *presents the authors' research into the new and lucrative connections between toy companies and the television industry. It also outlines how the elimination of government regulations in the 1980s allowed this partnership to come about, and contrasts war toys aimed at boys with the equally stereotypical toys marketed to girls.*

Congress recently took a small step toward wresting control over children's play from those who profit from it. A bill passed in October limits advertising during children's television shows and requires stations to run children's educational programs. However, the provisions of the new bill are much weaker than those that existed prior to deregulation. (Ronald Reagan vetoed a similar bill in

NANCY CARLSSON-PAIGE is associate professor of education at Lesley College Graduate School in Cambridge, Massachusetts. DIANE E. LEVIN is associate professor of education at Wheelock College in Boston. They are co-directors of the Lesley-Wheelock Peace Center and research associates at the Center for Psychological Studies in the Nuclear Age.

1988, and this fall George Bush refused to sign the present one, allowing it to pass into law without his signature.) Apparently, NBC didn't take the hint. Just before Congress passed the bill, NBC named the former head of marketing for Hasbro, Inc.—the maker of GI Joe—as the network's vice president of children's and family programs. ∎

The issue of war play and whether or not it is good for children has been a concern of parents for generations. The experiences of today's parents, however, are more intense than those of parents who raised their children prior to the 1980s.

One parent describes the dilemma she faces when her son asks her to play GI Joe with him. "I feel like I'm rejecting him if I say I won't do it," she says. "I feel like I'm fighting all the commercials, the ingenious advertising, all the stuff at Toys R Us, and I can't fight that."

In the past, children determined the content of their war play. They made guns out of whatever materials they could find and they invented pretend enemies using their imaginations. In doing so, they were in charge of their war play and the ideas they formed from it. In fact, war play has potential value. Perhaps more than any other form of dramatic play, war play is appealing because it allows children to feel powerful. At an age when children can feel helpless and out of control as they face such scary tasks as needing to separate from home and go to school or day care, this sense of having control and power can be very important. It is often children who are experiencing some difficult life event—such as parental divorce or a stay at a hospital—who seem most involved in war play.

But the war play of the last decade is fundamentally different from that which preceded it. Many of the ideas today do not come from children's own minds nor are they expressive of children's needs. They come from television and toys, and they come from the people who make them. It is difficult for children growing up now to bring their own ideas into their war play or to use play for their own self-defined ends. More often they use it to imitate the violence they have seen on television. And this is what makes today's breed of war play so worrisome.

PROGRAMMING CHILDREN

At no other time in history have children had daily exposure to so many images removed from daily experience, many of which focus on violence. Children's television offers far more hours of war cartoons than it did just a few years ago: more than 27 hours a week in 1988 compared with one-and-one-half hours a week in 1982. Beginning in 1987 a child could buy an expensive toy that, when used along with a television show, would "interact" electronically in a shooting match with the television set.

There is an accompanying proliferation of war toys on the market, most of which are linked to the television shows children watch. The sale of war toys has risen by more than 500% in the last four years, to well over $1 billion a year. The best-selling toy over the Christmas season for each of the past several years has been some kind of war toy: GI Joe for two consecutive years and last year, Nintendo video games, 80% of which are violent.

Toy manufacturers spend millions on television advertising targeted at children in an effort to influence their early consumer habits. By the age of 18, the average child growing up in the United States today will have seen between 350,000 and 640,000 television commercials.

The dramatic changes in media and toy culture that occurred in the 1980s follow from changes in federal regulations under the Reagan administration. Over a six-year period, the Federal Communications Commission (FCC), which governs the television industry, gradually nullified most of the regulations that once tried to assure quality programming

and control advertising aimed at children. Prior to the 1980s, the commission had said that programming was to come first, not the selling of products; it was illegal to market a toy with a television show. They had also placed a limit on the number of advertising minutes per hour permitted on children's television. But in 1984 the FCC eliminated these restrictions, making the "program-length commercial"—the marketing of toys as part of the program—legal for the first time and drastically increasing the amount of advertising.

The toy and television industries quickly joined together in determined marketing efforts. Toy manufacturers got into the business of making children's television shows for the first time as they began developing toys and programs as a package. The profits in toy sales were enormous, and some toy manufacturers began to share the wealth with television stations that carried their shows. By December 1985, all of the ten best-selling toys had television shows connected to them; and in the fall of 1987, 80% of all children's television programming was produced—literally paid for—by toy companies.

Sales of TV-linked toys skyrocketed

after deregulation, growing from $7 to $14 billion between 1980 and 1988. In 1984 alone, Mattell sold 35 million of the He-Man action figures; that meant 94,628 toy sales a day, or 66.4 every minute. Small toy companies that could not compete in the TV-dominated marketplace began to disappear. In a two-year period, Hasbro, the maker of GI Joe, took over Milton Bradley, Playskool, and CBS Toys.

WHOSE GAME IS THIS?

Because of the TV-toy link up, children increasingly were made to feel that they had to have certain toys in order to play. While in the past, children had grabbed whatever they could find for props to use in acting out stories they liked, now they were being told: "You should play GI Joe and to play it you need these action figures, these tanks, these props." This was a subtle but profound shift in the locus of control of play—away from children and into the hands of toy manufacturers. It undermined children's basic sense of self-sufficiency in play.

In addition, manufacturers were producing whole lines of toys paralleling what children were seeing in TV shows in order to increase profits. Every toy had one specific function so that a child would have to buy lots of them in order to play. The president of Hasbro stated that the GI Joe line, which has over 50 items, was designed to turn over completely every two years. This marketing strategy led children to begin to think in terms of quantities of toys. The emphasis in play shifted from "What can I do with this toy?" to "Can I get another one?" Toy supermarkets prospered, and for the first time people shopped for toys by filling up shopping carts.

Toys with one function, however, often leave children feeling unfulfilled. Once they've been used in the intended way and the novelty wears off, it's hard to figure out what to do with them next—how to use them in a creative and imaginative way. Children may end up experiencing feelings of deprivation, even as they sit among a vast array of toys.

The bulk of the war toys around today are too highly structured and realistic. Action figures such as the Master of the Universe character "Mosquitor" do one single grotesque thing. When the button on his back is pushed, the "blood" Mosquitor has "sucked" from his victims churns around in his transparent stomach in a very realistic way. Today's toy designers seem to be stretching their imaginations to new heights in trying to come up with novel functions for toys—looking for the new twist that will get children to want it, that will get children hooked.

To make matters worse, toy manufacturers and other companies that bought licenses to use a toy line's logo began to manufacture a variety of other products using the logo from the TV character. GI Joe sneakers, Rambo party plates, Care-Bear underwear, Transformer pajamas, and He-Man lunch boxes poured forth. In 1986, 51 companies were selling more than 120 products with the Transformer logo alone. Worse still, in the spring of 1990, more than 200 companies were licensed to produce over 1,000 products with the Teenage Mutant Ninja Turtle logo in preparation for the release of the movie.

Sometimes these products were not just for children; for example, Zip-loc bags appeared with the Transformer logo on them and a decal inside. The obvious goal was to manipulate children into asking for the product because of its logo.

And this practice worked. By 1986, the Toy Manufacturers of America estimated that close to 50% of the toy industry's sales were of licensed products. The toys, the television programs linked to them, and the products featuring the logos all became advertisements for each other.

SUGAR AND SPICE

While war toys have been aimed almost exclusively at boys, girls have proved just as ripe an audience for the new marketing strategies of toy manufacturers and television producers. In fact, what has emerged is a set of toys which are as stereotypically "female" as the fare being offered to boys is stereotypically "male."

The programs and toys developed for girls today have two central themes—feelings and appearance. The feelings theme focuses on "gentle" feelings such as caring, sharing, and nurturance, or sadness and helplessness. One example of a "feeling toy" line/television program is the "Care Bears." Each Care Bear has been assigned one specific personality trait by the manufacturer and always behaves according to that trait. The Care Bears define almost exclusively light and happy feelings. There is "Cheer Bear," "Tenderheart Bear," "Funshine Bear," and so on. Stronger emotions such as hostility and anger, along with the stronger actions that might accompany them, are reserved for boys' toys and television programs.

The other major theme found in the television programs and toys aimed at girls is appearance. Toy lines such as "Barbie" and "Jem" are typical examples. The focus of all of these dolls is on clothes, hairstyles, and make-up which reflect the latest fashions of the glamorous and affluent. Mattell, the manufacturer of the Barbie toy line, claims to be the world's largest producer of "women's wear" today. Only very narrow standards of beauty are imparted to girls through such toys, and little diversity in terms of ethnicity or body type. Barbie was the second best-selling toy line of the 1988 holiday season.

CALLING THE SHOTS

The new marketing climate permits manufacturers and advertisers to unleash techniques for capitalizing on children's vulnerabilities without restraint. As government withdrew from its protective role, whatever balance had existed among parents, government, and the TV/toy industries was profoundly disrupted. This imbalance allowed manufacturers to move in and profit while children and families paid the costs (the very situation the FCC was created to prevent). In this new equation, parents have been edged out. They have lost much of their previous control over their children's play culture.

In the last few years, efforts have been made to pass legislation that would reinstate some or all of the FCC regulations for children's television. Nevertheless, we see how far behind the United States is when we look at other countries. In Sweden, for example, consideration of children's play environments occurs at a national level, and responsibility for creating a healthy play culture is shared among government, business, and parents. The National Board for Consumer Policies, the Swedish Council for Children's Play, and the toy trade organizations have made a voluntary agreement to eliminate the advertising and sale of war toys depicting modern warfare from 1913 onward.

Finland has taken a similar approach. In 1986 the National Board for Social Welfare and the Entrepreneurs for Toy and Hobby Equipment Manufacturing signed an agreement to refrain from the manufacture, import and sale of war toys. Norway also has such an agreement.

Young children in the United States are now the target of sophisticated marketing strategies designed to exploit children and pressure parents. The new partnership between toy manufacturers and the television industry is transforming the way children play and the way children view the world. It has taken the control of children's play environment away from them and from their parents. Adults are left to wonder how much the toy industry's strategies will change their children's futures. ■

Who's Calling the Shots? was published in 1990 by New Society Publishers, an international publishing house with locations in Philadelphia, Santa Cruz, and Gabriola Island, British Columbia. For further information, call NSP toll free at 1-800-333-9093.

Dollars & Sense, June 1991

Enough Is Enough

Why more is not necessarily better than less

By Alan Durning

"Our enormously productive economy ... demands that we make consumption our way of life, that we convert the buying and use of goods into rituals, that we seek our spiritual satisfaction, our ego satisfaction, in consumption. ... We need things consumed, burned up, worn out, replaced, and discarded at an ever increasing rate."

Victor Lebow, U.S. retailing analyst, 1955

Across the country, Americans have responded to Victor Lebow's call, and around the globe, those who could afford it have followed. And many can: Worldwide, on average, a person today is four-and-a-half times richer than were his or her great-grandparents at the turn of the century.

Needless to say, that new global wealth is not evenly spread among the earth's people. One billion live in unprecedented luxury; one billion live in destitution.Overconsumption by the world's fortunate is an environmental problem unmatched in severity by anything except perhaps population growth. Surging exploitation of resources threatens to exhaust or unalterably disfigure forests, soils, water, air, and climate. High consumption may be a mixed blessing in human terms, too. Many in the industrial lands have a sense that, hoodwinked by a consumerist culture, they have been fruitlessly attempting to satisfy social, psychological, and spiritual needs with material things.

Of course, the opposite of over-consumption—poverty—is no solution to either environmental or human problems. It is infinitely worse for people and bad for the natural world. Dispossessed peasants slash and burn their way into Latin American rain forests, and hungry nomads turn their herds out onto fragile African range land, reducing it to desert. If environmental destruction results when people have either too little or too much, we are left to wonder how much is enough. What level of consumption can the earth support? When does having more cease to add appreciably to human satisfaction?

THE CONSUMING SOCIETY

Consumption is the hallmark of our era. The headlong advance of technology, rising earnings, and cheaper material goods have lifted consumption to levels never dreamed of a century ago. In the United States, the world's premier consuming society, people today on average own twice as many cars, drive two-and-a-half times as far, and travel 25 times further by air than did their parents in 1950. Air conditioning spread from 15% of households in 1960 to 64% in 1987, and color televisions from 1% to 93%. Microwave ovens and video cassette recorders reached almost two-thirds of American homes during the 1980s alone.

Japan and Western Europe have displayed parallel trends. Per person, the Japanese today consume more than four times as much aluminum, almost five times as much energy, and 25 times as much steel as they did in 1950. They also own four times as many cars and eat nearly twice as much meat. Like the Japanese, Western Europeans' consumption levels are only one notch below Americans'.

The late 1980s saw some poor societies begin the transition to consuming ways. In China, the sudden surge in spending on consumer durables shows up clearly in data from the State Statistical Bureau: Between 1982 and 1987, color televisions spread from 1% to 35% of urban Chinese homes, washing machines quadrupled from 16% to 67%, and refrigerators expanded their reach from 1% to 20%.

Meanwhile, in India, the emergence of a middle class, along with liberalization of the consumer market and the introduction of buying on credit, has led to explosive growth in sales of everything from automobiles and motorbikes to televisions and frozen dinners.

Few would begrudge anyone the simple advantages of cold food storage or mechanized clothes washing. The point, rather, is that even the oldest non-Western nations are emulating the high-consumption lifestyle. Long before all the world's people could achieve the American dream, however, we would lay waste the planet.

The industrial world's one billion meat eaters, car drivers, and throwaway consumers are responsible for the lion's share of the damage humans have caused common global resources.Over the past century, the economies of the wealthiest fifth of humanity have pumped out two-thirds of the greenhouse gases threatening the earth's climate, and each year their energy use releases three-fourths of the sulfur and nitrogen oxides causing acid rain. Their industries generate most of the world's hazardous chemical wastes, and their air conditioners, aerosol sprays, and factories release almost 90% of the chlorofluorocarbons destroying the earth's protective ozone layer. Clearly, even one billion profligate consumers is too much for the earth.

ALAN DURNING is a senior researcher at the Worldwatch Institute. This article is adapted from "Asking How Much Is Enough," Chapter Nine, in *State of the World*, 1991.

Beyond the environmental costs of acquisitiveness, some perplexing findings of social scientists throw doubt on the wisdom of high consumption as a personal and national goal: Rich societies have had little success in turning consumption into fulfillment. Regular surveys by the National Opinion Research Center of the University of Chicago reveal, for example, that no more Americans report they are "very happy" now than in 1957.

Likewise, a landmark study by sociologist Richard Easterlin in 1974 revealed that Nigerians, Filipinos, Panamanians, Yugoslavians, Japanese, Israelis, and West Germans all ranked themselves near the middle of a happiness scale. Confounding any attempt to correlate affluence and happiness, poor Cubans and rich Americans were both found to be considerably happier than the norm.

If the effectiveness of consumption in providing personal fulfillment is questionable, perhaps environmental concerns can help us redefine our goals.

IN SEARCH OF SUFFICIENCY

By examining current consumption patterns, we receive some guidance on what the earth can sustain. For three of the most ecologically important types of consumption—transportation, diet, and use of raw materials—the world's people are distributed unevenly over a vast range. Those at the bottom clearly fall below the "too little" line, while those at the top, in the cars-meat-and-disposables class, clearly consume too much.

Approximately one billion people do their traveling, aside from the occasional donkey or bus ride, on foot. Unable to get to jobs easily, attend school, or bring their complaints before government offices, they are severely hindered by the lack of transportation options.

Another three billion people travel by bus and bicycle. Kilometer for kilometer, bikes are cheaper than any other vehicle, costing less than $100 new in most of the Third World and requiring no fuel.

The world's automobile class is relatively small: Only 8% of humans, about 400 million people, own cars. The automobile makes itself indispensable: Cities sprawl, public transit atrophies, shopping centers multiply, workplaces scatter.

The global food consumption ladder has three rungs. According to the latest World Bank estimates, the world's 630 million poorest people are unable to provide themselves with a healthy diet. On the next rung, the 3.4 billion grain eaters of the world's middle class get enough calories and plenty of plant-based protein, giving them the world's healthiest basic diet.

The top of the ladder is populated by the meat eaters, those who obtain close to 40% of their calories from fat. These 1.25 billion people eat three times as much fat per person as the remaining four billion, mostly because they eat so much red meat. The meat class pays the price of its diet in high death rates from the so-called diseases of affluence—heart disease, stroke, and certain types of cancer.

The earth also pays for the high-fat diet. Indirectly, the meat-eating quarter of humanity consumes nearly 40% of the world's grain—grain that fattens the livestock they eat. Meat production is behind a substantial share of the environmental strains induced by agriculture, from soil erosion to overpumping of underground water.

In consumption of raw materials, such as steel, cotton, or wood, the same pattern emerges. A large group lacks many of the benefits provided by modest use of nonrenewable resources—particularly durables like radios, refrigerators, water pipes, tools, and carts with lightweight wheels and ball bearings. More than two billion people live in countries where per capita consumption of steel, the most basic modern material, falls below 50 kilograms a year.

Roughly 1.5 billion live in the middle class of materials use. Providing each of them with durable goods every year uses between 50 and 150 kilograms of steel. At the top of the heap is the industrial world or the throwaway class. A typical resident of the industrialized fourth of the world uses 15 times as much paper, 10 times as much steel, and 12 times as much fuel as a Third World resident.

In the throwaway economy, packaging becomes an end in itself, disposables proliferate, and durability suffers. Americans toss away 180 million razors annually, enough paper and plastic plates and cups to feed the world a picnic six times a year, and enough aluminum cans to make 6,000 DC-10 airplanes. Similarly, the Japanese use 30 million "disposable" single-roll cameras each year, and the British dump 2.5 billion diapers.

THE CULTIVATION OF NEEDS

What prompts us to consume so much? "The avarice of mankind is insatiable," wrote Aristotle 23 centuries ago. As each of our desires is satisfied, a new one appears in its place. All of economic theory is based on that observation.

What distinguishes modern consuming habits, some would say, is simply that we are much richer than our ancestors, and consequently have more ruinous effects on nature. While a great deal of truth lies in that view, five distinctly modern factors play a role in cultivating particularly voracious appetites: the influence of social pressures in mass societies, advertising, the shopping culture, vari-

> Many in the industrial lands have a sense that, hoodwinked by a consumerist culture, they have been fruitlessly attempting to satisfy social, psychological, and spiritual needs with material things.

33

ous government policies, and the expansion of the mass market into households and local communities.

In advanced industrial nations, daily interactions with the economy lack the face-to-face character prevailing in surviving local communities. Traditional virtues such as integrity, honesty, and skill are too hard to measure to serve as yardsticks of social worth. By default, they are gradually supplanted by a simple, single indicator—money. As one Wall Street banker put it bluntly to the *New York Times*, "Net worth equals self-worth."

Beyond social pressures, the affluent live completely enveloped in pro-consumption advertising messages. The sales pitch is everywhere. One analyst estimates that the typical American is exposed to 50-100 advertisements each morning before nine o'clock. Along with their weekly 22-hour diet of television, American teenagers are typically exposed to three to four hours of TV advertisements a week, adding up to at least 100,000 ads between birth and high school graduation.

Marketers have found ever more ways to push their products. Ads are piped into classrooms and doctors' offices, woven into the plots of feature films, placed on board games, mounted in bath-room stalls, and played back between rings on public phones in the Kansas City airport. Even the food supply may go mass media: The Viskase company of Chicago now offers to print edible ad slogans on hot dogs, and Eggverts International is using a similar technique to advertise on thousands of eggs in Israel.

Advertising has been one of the fastest growing industries during the past half-century. In the United States, ad expenditures rose from $198 per capita in 1950 to $498 in 1989. Worldwide, over the same period, per person advertising expenditures grew from $15 to $46. In developing countries, the increases have been astonishing. Advertising billings in India jumped fivefold in the 1980s; newly industrialized South Korea's advertising industry grew 35-40% annually in the late 1980s.

Shopping, particularly in the United States, seems to have become a primary cultural activity. Americans spend six hours a week shopping. Some 93% of American teenage girls surveyed in 1987 deemed shopping their favorite pastime.

Government policies also play a role in promoting consumption and in worsening its ecological impact. The British tax code, for example, encourages businesses to buy thousands of large com-pany cars for employee use. Most governments in North and South America subsidize beef production on a massive scale.

Finally, the sweeping advance of the commercial mass market into realms once dominated by family members and local enterprise has made consumption far more wasteful than in the past. More and more, flush with cash but pressed for time, households opt for the questionable "conveniences" of prepared, packaged foods, miracle cleaning products, and disposable everything—from napkins to shower curtains. All these things cost the earth dearly, and change households from productive units of the economy to passive, consuming entities.

Like the household, the community economy has atrophied—or been dismembered—under the blind force of the money economy. Shopping malls, superhighways, and strips have replaced corner stores, local restaurants, and neighborhood theaters—the very places that help create a sense of common identity and community. Traditional Japanese vegetable stands and fish shops are giving way to supermarkets and convenience stores, and styrofoam and plastic film have replaced yesterday's newspaper as fish wrap.

All these things nurture the acquisitive desires that everyone has. Can we, as individuals and as citizens, act to confront these forces?

THE CULTURE OF PERMANENCE

The basic value of a sustainable society, the ecological equivalent of the Golden Rule, is simple: Each generation should meet its own needs without jeopardizing the prospects of future generations to meet theirs.

For individuals, the decision to live a life of sufficiency—to find their own answer to the question "how much is enough?"—is to begin a highly personal process. Social researcher Duane Elgin estimated in 1981—perhaps optimistically—that 10 million adult Americans were experimenting "wholeheartedly" with voluntary simplicity. India, the Netherlands, Norway, Western Germany, and the United Kingdom all have small segments of their populations who adhere to a non-consuming philosophy. Motivated by the desire to live justly in an unjust world, to walk gently on the earth, and to avoid distraction, clutter, and pretense, their goal is not ascetic self-denial but personal fulfillment. They do not think consuming more is likely to provide it.

Realistically, voluntary simplicity is unlikely to gain ground rapidly against the onslaught of consumerist values. And, ultimately, personal restraint will do little if not wedded to bold political and social steps against the forces promoting consumption. Commercial television, for example, will need fundamental reorientation in a culture of permanence. As religious historian Robert Bellah put it, "That happiness is to be attained through limitless material acquisition is denied by every religion and philosophy known to humankind, but is preached incessantly by every American television set."

Direct incentives for overconsumption are also essential targets for reform. If goods' prices reflected something closer to the environmental cost of their production, through revised subsidies and tax systems, the market itself would guide consumers toward less damaging forms of consumption. Disposables and packaging would rise in price relative to durable, less-packaged goods; local unprocessed food would fall in price relative to prepared products trucked from far away.

The net effect might be lower overall consumption as people's effective purchasing power declined. As currently constituted, unfortunately, economies penalize the poor when aggregate consumption contracts: Unemployment skyrockets and inequalities grow. Thus arises one of the greatest challenges for sustainable economics in rich societies— finding ways to ensure basic employment opportunities for all without constantly stoking the fires of economic growth.

In the final analysis, accepting and living by sufficiency rather than excess offers a return to what is, culturally speaking, the human home: to the ancient order of family, community, good work, and good life; to a reverence for excellence of skilled handiwork; to a true materialism that does not just care about things but cares for them; to communities worth spending a lifetime in. The very things that make life worth living, that give depth and bounty to human existence, are infinitely sustainable. ■

Dollars & Sense, January/February 1992

All Work & No Play

A conversation with Juliet Schor on the "spend and work" ethic

Juliet Schor *is the author of* **The Overworked American**, *to be released by Basic Books in January. In her book, Schor traces the rising number of hours Americans work, and looks at the causes— and possible solutions— for overwork.*

Schor is an associate professor of economics and a member of the Committee on Degrees in Women's Studies at Harvard University. She has also taught for the Center for Popular Economics since its founding. **Dollars & Sense** *Collective Member* **Chris Tilly** *interviewed her in October.* ■

What has happened to paid per capita work hours since the 1940s?

They've risen quite substantially. In the 1950s and 1960s, there was very little change in paid working hours. But since the end of the 1960s, there's been a steady upward creep in paid hours in the United States. I've looked at the average person with a job who is not unemployed or working part-time involuntarily during the year. Since 1969, the average increase for this group is 138 hours a year.

It's not just the groups you would expect to work longer hours who are doing so. For example, it's not just women, though women are working much longer paid hours—on average about two months more a year. Men are also working more hours, up by two and one-half weeks a year. The people at the top of the income distribution are working more, the people in the middle are working more, and the people at the bottom are working more. There is more

overtime and moonlighting, and people are working a greater fraction of the year. Professionals are putting in longer hours. All of these are combining to give us longer hours.

You have described this trend as surprising. Why is that?

Over this whole 40-year period, from the Second World War until now, American economic progress, in the form of productivity growth, gave us as a nation the opportunity to cut our paid work time in half. We can now produce our 1948 standard of living in less than half the time it took back then. So we could have had a 20-hour week or we could have had people working one year on, one year off with pay. If we look at the 70 or 80 years before 1948, there was a dramatic decline in working hours, basically through a reduction in the work day, and economic progress was channeled into fewer working hours. That stopped after World War II completely.

So it is surprising in light of our own history. It is also surprising when you look at Europe, which was following a similar trajectory to ours in the second half of the 19th century and the first half of the 20th century. In Europe they continued to reduce working hours after the Second World War, so that now hours are considerably lower in Europe—workers receive four to six weeks of paid vacation a year, and the working week has been shortened in some countries.

Why did the United States follow

such a different path?

One reason is our relatively weak trade unions. The earlier reduction of hours in the United States came about in large part because of a vigorous union struggle. After the Second World War, the union movement in this country basically abandoned the goal of shorter hours. Of course, unions are also weaker here than in Europe. So even if they had maintained this goal, they might have been less successful in getting shorter hours. The differences in the strength of the union movement have been important, for example, in the ability to get paid vacation and also in the ability to get some of these things passed into law so that they apply to all workers. We don't have a nationally

don't have enough time outside of work. Marriages where you have one or both partners working very long hours are under a lot of strain. People cite not having enough time to be with the family as one of their most serious social problems. Volunteer work and community service are also getting squeezed out by this rise in paid work.

Mainstream economists would say people choose how many hours to work. How would you respond to this?

Let's look at why people are working more. For the people at the top, in the glamorous white collar professions, you can say, yes, they're choosing these hours because nobody is forcing them to take

sition to capitalism, they needed to work those hours just to survive. In some ways, it was similar to what I was just describing for the present.

So, capitalism brought a dramatic long-term increase in the hours that people work. Then, somewhere in the middle of the 19th century the hours started to fall, largely due to labor organizing. By the time you get to the end of the Second World War, in some sense you're back to where you were in the Middle Ages. People say, isn't capitalism great? It has given us all this leisure. But that's only if you ignore the earlier history.

Why do present-day employers have an interest in extending work hours?

One important thing is the way fringe benefits such as health insurance are paid. Because they are paid on a per person basis, not a per hour basis, employers like it when their workers work longer hours. So if we had, for example, national health insurance, I think it would be easier to reduce hours.

Also, for any given hourly wage, long hours at any one employer lead people to be more dependent on that employer. They are getting more income from that employer, so it is more costly to lose that job. By extending working hours, employers can get more labor discipline without raising the hourly wage.

Plus, we still have lots of people who are on fixed salaries that do not increase when they work long hours. These tend to be in the higher-paying jobs.

The work ethic, which is very strong here compared to Europe, has become not just a work ethic but also a consumption ethic.

---

mandated vacation, the way they do in many European countries.

The other reason is cultural. We in the United States are a more consumerist and more materialist society than a lot of these European countries. People tend to spend money rather than trying to get free time. The work ethic, which is very strong here compared to Europe, has come to be not just a work ethic but also a consumption ethic. Consumerism is the carrot to go with the stick of the work ethic; it has allowed people to accept the very long hours they have to work.

What's so bad about people working a lot?

Work is a good thing. But we've lost the balance between different types of work—paid work versus work in the home and volunteer work—and also between work and leisure time. Probably the most serious problem that we face is the degradation of family life, the difficulties that parents are having taking care of their children, for example, because they just

these jobs. But to hold those jobs, the hours that you have to put in have been rising. So in that sense it is not a choice.

For the bottom 80% of the labor force, wages have fallen by so much in the last 20 years that in order for workers to maintain their former standard of living, they would have to put in about 250 additional hours a year.

Haven't you also argued that in general capitalism creates pressures for increased market hours?

If you look at capitalism, from its origins in the Middle Ages to the mid-19th century, the growth of the market economy and wage labor led to much longer working hours, an increase of between a third and in some cases even a doubling of hours. Part of it was employers trying to increase profits, because people were paid on a daily basis and they didn't typically get more money if the employer was able to extend the day. At the same time, with the degradation of conditions for large numbers of people in the tran-

How have changes in paid work time differed for men and women, and how have hours of housework changed?

Men still work much longer hours in the market than women do, although that gap is narrowing. Total hours, including household and market hours, are much closer.

In the last 20 years, among the population as a whole, unpaid domestic hours declined by 60 hours a year per person. The decline for women was very large, about 244 hours a year. The rise for men was about 161. So there was some decline in household hours, but it didn't offset the rise in market hours.

Now that's for the population as a whole. Among people in the labor force, women are doing less household work but men are doing more, so it cancels out.

Why didn't all the improvements in housework technology lead to a bigger reduction in hours spent in housework?

If you look from the 1910s to the late 1970s, there is no reduction in the average weekly hours that a full-time housewife puts in. This is astounding when you think about all the labor-saving technology—vacuum cleaners, washing machines, and so on— that has gone into the household during that time. All of the conveniences to lighten the workload of the housewife didn't lighten it.

My view is that it has to do with economic incentives. Housewives were basically full-time in the home, with very few opportunities for earning income outside the home, and they didn't get paid. There was no economic incentive to conserve their labor. So as all of these devices came in, which allowed them to spend less time at housework, they ended up producing more and more services:

> There is still great resistance from business to shorter hours. What you hear from business is that in order to compete, Americans have to work long hours.

cleaner houses, cleaner clothes, fancier food, spending more time with the kids. It's the same point I was making about all the productivity that we've had in the paid economy. We could have taken more leisure time; instead, we put it into increased output. The housewife did the same thing.

It isn't until women start going into the labor force in a big way that labor-saving devices do contribute to the reduction of labor time. Because when a woman starts working in the market, she does cut back on work at home.

So what do you think it will take to solve all of these work time problems?

In public opinion polls, people increasingly say they want more time outside of their paid jobs. A recent Hilton Hotels poll showed, for example, that even large numbers of people making $20,000 a year or less are willing to give up a day's pay for additional time off— that's astounding. Among those earning $30,000 and up, something like half of the people are saying they would make that trade-off. So the desire for time off is operating among both lower-paid and higher paid people. Other polls show eight out of ten people saying they would forgo a faster-track career—higher paying, more glamorous, more promotions— in order to spend more time with family. This holds for large majorities of both men and women.

But there is still great resistance from business to shorter hours. What you hear from business is that in order to compete with the Japanese, Americans have to work long hours.

So public opinion is not going to be powerful unless people organize. Where there are unions, workers need to push the unions to deal with this. The 80-plus percent of the work force that doesn't have unions has to start getting together in small groups at their workplaces and start to challenge their employers. Women's groups need to take this up. So do environmental groups, because we need to stop growing so quickly and producing so much stuff that's dangerous for

Rising work hours

Annual work hours of unconstrained labor force *

	1969	1973	1979	1989	Change 1969-89
Paid Hours					
Men	2054	2060	2093	2126	72
Women	1406	1436	1558	1693	287
Average**	1786	1798	1855	1924	138
Unpaid Domestic Hours					
Men	621	626	727	688	67
Women	1268	1248	1204	1142	-126
Average**	889	888	939	900	11
Total Hours					
Men	2675	2686	2820	2814	139
Women	2674	2584	2762	2835	161
Average**	2675	2686	2794	2824	149

* The unconstrained labor force consists of both full-time and part-time people who are working all the hours they wish to work. Part-time workers who would prefer more hours are not included.
** This average is weighted to account for different numbers of men and women in the labor force.

Source: Juliet Schor's calculations based on numbers from the *Current Population Survey* and Michigan Time-Use Data.

the environment, and one way to do that is to start taking progress in the form of free time.

What does a program of shorter hours mean for the poorest people, who aren't working enough at this point?

One thing we haven't talked about is the 20% of the workforce who are unable to get the hours they want, who are unemployed or underemployed. For those people, a top priority is to allow them to get the hours they want. That involves government commitment to full employment and programs designed to enhance employment.

Another thing: For the people at the bottom of the occupational ladder, shorter hours are not feasible because their incomes are too low. Those people need increases in hourly wages to allow them the opportunity to opt for more time off. At the moment, with such a large percentage of the work force earning wages that don't even bring them out of poverty, it is utopian to talk about them trading off income for time. That's why a comprehensive program for shortening work hours would address wages, unemployment and hours of work together.

Are there specific policy reforms you think could be the basis for a movement on work time?

Government-mandated paid vacation is something I think everyone can get behind, with the exception of business. Particularly now: In the last ten years, vacation and other paid time off has shrunk in this economy by about 15%.

Has your research ended up changing your work time?

Well, of course, when I was writing the book, I worked harder than I ever have in my life. And I always thought it was a great irony. But I'm trying to make up for that now.

I feel it has changed me. My own views about work and the kind of work schedules that are sane, and the kind of work schedule that I would like to follow in my life, have been changed by writing this book. I used to be the kind of person who felt she should be working all the time, and I'm trying not to be that kind of person any more. ■

Dollars & Sense, October 1991

Psst... Need a Loan?

Banks' discriminatory practices push consumers into second mortgage scams

By Peter Dreier

The 1987 comedy film "Tin Men" depicted fast-talking aluminum-siding salesmen in early 1960s Baltimore. Using clever scams, these salesmen enticed lower middle-class homeowners to purchase their product.

Three decades later, con artists still operate in working-class neighborhoods in cities around the United States, targeting elderly, poor, and minority homeowners. These hustlers work primarily for small construction contractors who promise to make home improvements, such as replacing wood boards with vinyl siding, installing new windows, or fixing rotting porches. In many cases, the contractor's work is shoddy or never completed.

The contractors and their salespeople often work in tandem with private mortgage companies that offer exorbitant loan terms and fees. Homeowners often wind up going deeply in debt, and some even lose their houses to foreclosure.

John Storms is one such victim. Storms needed a loan to install handicapped access ramps for his 22-year-old foster daughter in his home in Boston's

Roxbury neighborhood. Contractors charged Storms an estimated five times the market price for the work. Way over his head in debt, Storms refinanced the loan several times, but eventually lost his house when the mortgage company foreclosed.

A 1989 report by the American Association of Retired Persons (AARP) found that private mortgage and home-improvement con artists have hit homeowners across the country. The Landmark Equity Co., for example, made 10,000 mortgages between 1982 and 1985 in Virginia, Maryland, Alabama, Georgia, and South Carolina, many of them to elderly homeowners. These loans involved a variety of deceptive and fraudulent practices, according to the AARP. Within three years, an estimated 30% to 70% of the mortgages were in default. In cases involving other companies in Chicago, Atlanta, New York, Newark, and other cities, attorneys have filed class-action suits against contractors and mortgage companies.

In Boston, reporters, community activists, and government officials recently uncovered one more culprit in second-mortgage scams: mainstream banks. The movie "Tin Men" portrayed the hustlers as small-time entrepreneurs on the margins of legitimate business. But in Roxbury and other Boston neighborhoods the scandal is linked to the broader problem of "redlining."

A bank redlines when it refuses to open branches or provide credit in low-

PETER DREIER is a director of housing at the Boston Redevelopment Authority, housing policy adviser to Boston Mayor Ray Flynn, and an editor of *Shelterforce*, a publication for housing activists sponsored by the National Housing Institute in Orange, N.J.

income, usually black, neighborhoods. This practice has left a vacuum for conventional credit that makes homeowners vulnerable to mortgage hustlers. Some banks also profit by extending credit to the contractors and private mortgage firms.

The problem in Boston attracted particular attention because the local press, as well as community and local government leaders, worked hard to uncover and resolve the plight of victims and linked the problem to powerful mainstream banks. No one yet knows how many Boston homeowners may have been suckered, but estimates range from hundreds to thousands.

HOUSE RICH, CASH POOR

Not all home improvement loans (also known as home equity loans or second mortgages) are scams. Nor is every private mortgage company shady. Every day, thousands of people take out legitimate second mortgages from banks and private mortgage companies across the country. Many major bank-holding companies have mortgage-company subsidiaries. But when homeowners can not get conventional loans at a bank to fix their property, whole neighborhoods become vulnerable to the unsavory side of the second-mortgage and home-improvement industries.

Mortgage companies specialize in selling second mortgages to homeowners who can not obtain loans from mainstream banks. As a whole, these companies are not as closely regulated as conventional banks and thrifts, so they operate with little scrutiny of their fees and business practices and few controls over interest rates. In Massachusetts, for example, state law does not impose any upper limit on interest rates for mortgages on properties worth more than $40,000. Because the vast majority of houses are valued at more than $40,000, con artists thrive in this unregulated environment.

Home-improvement scams work in various ways. The borrower, typically a resident of a redlined neighborhood, may have applied for a loan at the bank to replace old windows, but the bank turned down her request. Because the homeowner still needs money to fix the windows, she may approach a mortgage

ILLUSTRATIONS BY MARGARET FAULK

company that lends in the neighborhood without knowing whether the company is legitimate or not.

Mortgage brokers and home-repair contractors also visit neighborhoods and identify houses that need repairs. They then approach the homeowners by stopping by the house or phoning. If a salesperson or a broker makes the contact, that person will often offer to hook the homeowner up with a contractor. Or a contractor might approach first, and offer to arrange the loan with a bank or broker.

Salespersons, brokers, and contractors all promise borrowers good terms on the loans. But unscrupulous mortgage companies actually charge high and deceptive interest rates and/or inflated fees. Interest rates can run as high as 40%, while a home equity loan from a mainstream Boston bank now goes for around 11%. A laundry list of fees, some of which are hidden until after the loan is completed, add to the cost. After all this, the borrowers often never see any money, because it goes directly from the mortgage company to the home-improvement contractor.

In addition, false information about loan applicants' income and employment sometimes appears on loan applications after homeowners sign the forms. By falsifying data, the second-mortgage company is more likely to be able to later sell the loan to a mainstream bank. For example, Storms is an 81-year-old black man with a monthly income of $493. His loan

application for Northeastern Mortgage Company listed him as a 60-year-old white male, the owner of a day-care business and a social worker with a monthly salary of $1,675. Storms says he never saw the falsified form and has no idea how the wrong information was listed.

Why do contractors and mortgage companies target poor people? With homes as their only large asset, low-income homeowners go to extraordinary lengths (including taking second and third jobs) to pay back their loans, and will pay as long as they can to prevent foreclosure. In addition, contractors and lenders realize that the potential scam victims are "house rich, but cash poor." In Boston's hot housing market of the 1980s, their homes became valuable property, even in predominantly low-income neighborhoods in Dorchester, Roxbury, and Mattapan. If a consumer misses payments, the mortgage company can foreclose, take over the house, and sell it.

Thomas and Mattie Middleton, both handicapped and in their late 70s, lost their home that way. Homeowners in Roxbury, the Middletons had paid off the entire mortgage on their modest three-family house when they took out a second mortgage. A contractor brought them a loan document to sign from Growth Mortgage Co., a Brookline, Massachusetts firm. The firm provided a $99,792 loan with a 24% interest rate. This translated into $2,062 in monthly payments, an impossible burden for a couple with about $800 in monthly income. The president of Growth Mortgage Co. says the contractor convinced him that the Middletons could have met the payments by renting two units after the renovations were completed. The contractor never finished the repairs, and was unreachable when the Middletons tried to contact him. Growth Mortgage foreclosed on the loan, taking the Middletons' house—which they bought in 1962 for $15,500—and reselling it for $134,000.

THE ROLE OF BANKS

Mortgage companies like Growth Mortgage profited from Boston home-improvement scams along with contractors. In addition, mainstream banks not only fueled the problem by redlining these neighborhoods but also profited by doing business with the con-artist contractors and fast-buck finance firms.

"We make a living at this because the bankers don't serve these people," Carl Paolucci, president of Eastbay Financial Services, a mortgage broker, told the *Boston Globe*. "The bankers created an opportunity for the broker."

Banks profit by providing business loans to the home-improvement contractors and mortgage companies. Research by the *Boston Globe*, Channel 7 WNEV-TV, and the Union Neighborhood Assistance Corporation (UNAC), an offshoot of the hotel workers' union, found that several New England banks extended lines of credit to mortgage companies engaging in deceptive practices. These investigations have not yet revealed the extent of the banks' knowledge of the mortgage companies' unethical conduct.

New England's major commercial banks also profited by purchasing these high-interest mortgages from the private mortgage firms. Second mortgage companies sell their mortgages either individually or in bundles to mainstream banks. In return, the banks give the mortgage companies cash that they can use to sell more second mortgages. The Bank of New England, for example, one of the largest banks in the region at the time, purchased high-interest mortgages from Growth Mortgage Co. and also gave the company a $10 million line of credit. In some cases, the same bank that turns down a homeowner's mortgage request later buys that homeowner's loan from a private mortgage company.

Nationwide, 12% of large banks buy second mortgages from private lenders, reports the Virginia-based Consumer Bankers' Association. Ironically, some banks cite their purchase of second mortgages in minority communities as evidence that they are fulfilling the mandates of the federal Community Reinvestment Act (CRA)—the law that requires banks receiving deposits from a neighborhood to provide banking services and credit to its residents.

ACTIVISTS MOBILIZE, POLITICIANS RESPOND

Boston's community activists and elected officials demanded that banks participating in the home-improvement scams compensate victims. To put pressure on lenders, several African-American community organizations and UNAC are planning individual and class-action lawsuits against contractors, mortgage companies, and banks.

At first, Boston-area banks denied complicity in the mortgage scam. The Massachusetts Bankers' Association, the industry lobby group, opposed calls by activists and elected officials for a statewide moratorium on foreclosures, then called for banks to participate in a voluntary moratorium, and finally supported legislation for a mandatory 120-day freeze to allow time to sort out the problem. The state legislature passed the freeze in July.

Fleet/Norstar was the first bank to acknowledge its role in the scam. At the time, Fleet had an application pending with the federal government to purchase the failed Bank of New England, a bid that was later approved. Under pressure from Boston Mayor Ray Flynn, Fleet/Norstar agreed to compensate victims. Other banks began negotiations with community activists, although, as of August, only Fleet/Norstar had put money on the table.

Activists and politicians called for changes in the CRA as well as in state regulation of home-improvement contractors and private mortgage companies. The U.S. Senate and House banking committees came to Boston for a public hearing and pledged to close CRA loopholes so that banks will be penalized instead of rewarded for such practices. And Mayor Flynn and others sponsored a bill in the state legislature to put a ceiling on interest rates and fees for home-improvement loans. The mortgage-company regulation bill was passed quickly, but the other legislative initiatives are still in limbo.

Until June, Massachusetts was one of the few states that did not regulate mortgage companies and brokers. But even in states that do, mortgage scams continue. Often the laws are not strong enough, or the state agencies fail to enforce them. But regulating these firms, as well as home-improvement contractors, is only a small part of the solution. Perhaps even more important are state regulations making usurious loans illegal. States with such laws—such as Arkansas, Texas, and North Carolina—have effectively put a limit on price-gouging second mortgages.

The fundamental remedy for home improvement scams is to eliminate redlining. During the past several years, studies in a number of cities across the country, including Boston, have demonstrated that lenders continue to discriminate against low-income and minority neighborhoods.

Ironically, just as the Boston media were exposing the mortgage scam and the banks' role in it, the nation's banking industry was pressuring Congress to effectively kill the CRA. Community activists, unions, clergy groups, consumer advocates, and big-city mayors mounted a counter-offensive during the summer to protect the CRA from attacks sponsored by legislators in the pockets of the banking lobby. As of late August, these efforts had successfully derailed anti-CRA amendments in the two banking committees, but the industry could still win at a later stage.

Meanwhile, as bankers and activists wage war over the CRA, a new generation of "tin men" continues to knock on the doors of homeowners in neighborhoods across America. ■

RESOURCES: *Boston Globe*, May-August 1991; *Consumer Problems with Home Equity Scams, Second Mortgages, and Home Equity Lines of Credit*, American Association of Retired Persons, Washington, DC, 1989.

Firms and Market Structure

Dollars & Sense, March 1992

Farm Policy for Whom?

Saving small farmers and boosting competition—NOT!

By Chris Williams

On New Year's Day 1991, Goran Jenson's family, coming in from homes scattered across the country, convened to discuss the future of their family farm. Settled 120 years ago by their Scandinavian ancestors, the 35-acre dairy farm on the outskirts of a small Wisconsin town has been home to four generations of Jensons. Raw Norwegian stubbornness—and a lot of luck—saw the family through the Great Depression and the mass farm foreclosures of the 1980s. Yet, that New Year's Day, the decision at hand was whether to continue farming. Younger Jensons questioned whether milk sales could support the farm for another year.

Hundreds of thousands of other owners of small and medium farms face the same decision. Since 1958, an estimated two million farms have closed. Between 1974 and 1987, about 370,000 small and medium farms shut down, many of them lost to foreclosure. Owners of larger farms snatched up many of the failed farms, creating about 135,000 new large farms during the same period.

These new large-scale farms joined the ranks of agro-chemical companies, food processors, traders, marketers, and other players in the farm industry that have been molding farm policy to corporate interests for three decades. Together, these business interests have overshadowed efforts by small farmers to shape government farm policies. As a result, price support systems designed in the 1930s to help family farmers now push them out of business and promote the growth of agribusiness.

HELP FOR FARMERS?

Government relief to farmers began in the 1870s, when it gave ad hoc financial assistance to farmers struck by drought or short on money for equipment, seed, and fertilizer. This support helped farmers strapped for cash, but it did not mitigate the price crashes brought about by periodic bumper crops.

The federal government intervened in farming more formally in the 1930s, when the Depression and natural disasters devastated family farming. In 1932, the Agricultural Adjustment Act (AAA) introduced farm price supports with other New Deal policies to stabilize wages and prices. The government paid farmers, stored food in federally controlled stocks, and then sold the food to traders and processors. This protected many farmers from price crashes and gave them immediate cash at harvest time.

Every four to five years, Congress revised the prices for each farm product in an amendment to the AAA commonly referred to as the Farm Bill. Initially, legislators determined prices by estimat-

CHRIS WILLIAMS is a *Dollars & Sense* Collective member.

Since 1958, an estimated two million U.S. farms have closed.

41

ing the cost of farm inputs and keying prices to costs. But in the early 1960s, Congress changed its criteria for price-setting. Legislators started setting prices below farmers' cost of production, in part to promote U.S. food exports. Congress,

Traders purchase food and fiber commodities at the government-mandated price and in turn trade them to processors on the open market. Processors turn the livestock and grains into consumer items, then sell the goods to wholesalers,

Large grain producers are often linked financially through mergers or joint ventures with traders and processors of grain, and agro-chemical corporations or the big four processors own some large farms. For example, Cargill, the world's largest privately owned corporation, is also the largest grain company and dominates hog slaughtering, wheat flour milling, wet corn milling, and beef processing.

Promoters of consolidation in the farm industry usually offer one of two rationalizations for pushing smaller farmers out to make way for agribusiness. The first is that consolidation is part of the natural evolution of industrialization and characteristic of a modern economy. The second is that consolidated firms are the most efficient and productive players in a market economy.

Low prices grease the wheels of just about everyone in the farming industry except small- and medium-sized farmers.

cognizant of farmers' loss of revenues, then introduced a formal subsidy structure. Today, price "supports" have little relation to actual production costs.

Since then, public discussions of federal farm policy have focused more on the size of subsidies than on price supports. In theory, subsidies are payments made to farmers to make up for the gap between the mandated prices and the farmers' costs of production. In reality, because costs are not a central consideration in setting prices, subsidies frequently do not make up the difference. Fluctuating property taxes, debt payments, and prices for seed, equipment, fertilizers, pesticides, and other inputs are frequently not met by commensurate increases in price rates.

Nonfarmers often think of subsidies as a hand-out, a gift of benevolence from the taxpayer to the farmer. This fails to consider that subsidies would be unnecessary if government-mandated prices covered farmers' costs.

The real beneficiaries of U.S. farm policy are not farmers, but large corporate interests further down the food production chain. Mark Ritchie of the Institute of Agriculture and Trade Policy, a Minneapolis-based policy group, says, "The [beneficiary] is often the buyer/trader, processor, marketer, all of whom benefit from a low buying price, while the farmer is still unable to cover costs."

Low prices grease the wheels of just about everyone in the farming industry except small- and medium-sized farmers.

who sell the goods to retailers. Low prices for the initial farm products keep down costs, and therefore boost profits for traders, processors, and marketers.

Companies in the pre-farm production sector also benefit from cheap farm prices. Fertilizer and pesticide manufacturers, for example, are strong advocates of low prices for food and fiber. Low prices force farmers to grow more to cover costs. To increase their per-acre crop yields, farmers fertilize their fields and use pesticides to ward off insects. The market for yield-boosting products is huge; chemicals comprise one-third of the cost of producing most food.

Many owners of large farms advocate cheap prices, as well, particularly hog and poultry farmers who purchase large amounts of grain for feed. These farmers sustain strong profits because their major inputs—grain, soy, and corn feed—are priced so cheaply.

Large grain farmers do not directly benefit from cheap prices, but they survive them better than smaller farmers thanks in part to diverse portfolios and access to capital. Many mega-farms are subsidiaries of large corporations, which use portions of farm land for condo developments, golf courses, or small manufacturing plants to cushion losses from low price rates. Large farms also benefit from economies of scale not available to smaller farms: They purchase inputs in bulk at low rates.

These farm industry players are not always separate entities; many firms that benefit from low prices are inter-related.

THE ROOTS OF CONSOLIDATION

Either way, farmers have to get out of the way. As economist Kenneth Boulding wrote in 1974, "The only way I know to get toothpaste out of a tube is to squeeze, and the only way to get people out of agriculture is likewise to squeeze agriculture."

Many people and organizations with influence over federal farm policy advocated this strategy in the early 1960s, including the Committee for Economic Development (CED). A private organization established in 1942 by presidents of several large corporations and economists from the University of Chicago, CED members included food and fiber processors, academics (many with board memberships in the industry), former U.S. Department of Agriculture (USDA) civil servants, and 200 machine, tool and seed manufacturers.

The main problems in agriculture, from CED's perspective, were declining profit margins and "excess resources" (that is, farmers). Capital-intensive farming, CED argued, would increase profits. In addition, lower prices for farm products would improve foreign sales of U.S. farm commodities.

In 1962, CED released "An Adaptive Program for Agriculture," one of a series of policy papers on agriculture. In it, CED called for moving one-third of the farm population out of farming within five years. To accomplish this, CED recommended immediately reducing price supports for wheat, cotton, rice, and other grains.

It is difficult to document how much this report influenced Congressional consideration of farm policy in the early 1960s. Many CED members did, however, hold key positions in the Eisenhower, Kennedy, and subsequent administrations. For example, Dale Hathaway, a Michigan State University economist and a key author of the CED report, served on the President's Council of Economic Advisors in 1955-56 and 1961-63. Jimmy Carter later appointed him assistant secretary of agriculture with responsibility for overseeing farm price support programs. According to Ritchie, Hathaway later worked with the South Korean government to relocate that nation's farmers to cities in order to create a larger urban labor pool.

In any case, U.S. policy followed the general direction CED desired. Government-mandated farm prices steadily slipped farther and farther below the cost of production, helping push 1.5 million farmers off the land by 1974, when roughly 25% of farms produced 80% of all farm products. Displaced farmers poured into urban labor markets, depressing real wages in many other industries (yet another goal of the 1962 CED report).

In the early 1970s, agribusiness advocated replacing subsidies with welfare payments to farmers. A 1974 CED report argued, "Assistance for farmers should be extended not through special support programs but rather through the same kind of program that should be made available to all disadvantaged Americans, urban or rural–i.e. through national welfare assistance programs." This approach would add to the pressures pushing small farmers out of business, because subsidies support small farming, while welfare doesn't.

Despite pressure from agribusiness, Congress has not implemented this recommendation. But in most cases, subsidies remain insufficient to cover farmers' costs of production. Farm Bill debates continue to ignore the more central issue of pricing.

The Reagan and early Bush administrations maintained anti-farmer farm policies, further increasing concentration of ownership of farming enterprises. Between 1974 and 1987, 175,000 small farms and 190,000 medium farms went out of business, and 125,000 large farms and 15,000 mega-farms were created. One prominent rural sociologist, William Heffernan of the University of Missouri, draws a parallel between farm consolidation and growing conglomeration of other industries. "The food sector is not behaving differently from the rest of the economic system," Heffernan observed in 1988. "One might say that the food sector is joining the rest of the economic system."

Heffernan documented 160 mergers, buyouts or joint investments between 1980 and 1988 in the markets for poultry, eggs, beef, hogs, feed grains, and soybeans. Food processing is particularly consolidated; four firms dominate most of the slaughtering and cutting of meats and preparation of grains. Heffernan

In most cases, subsidies remain insufficient to cover farmers' costs of production.

found, for example, that Occidental Petroleum, ConAgra, and Excell (a subsidiary of Cargill) currently control 75% of the nation's beef processing. Cargill and ADM Milling Company control roughly 55% of soybean processing.

FARM POLICY GOES GLOBAL

Today, agribusiness is working to change U.S. farm policy by working through a political arena outside Congressional control, the General Agreement on Tariffs and Trade (GATT). Initiated in 1986 in Uruguay, GATT is a series of negotiations among trade officials representing 100 countries. Negotiators are debating the terms of, and barriers to, more than 80% of the world's trade. Agricultural prices and subsidies are chief among the issues negotiators are debating.

U.S. agribusiness is no stranger to GATT negotiations. Daniel Amstutz, former USDA officer and a former senior vice-president of Cargill, is a member of the Bush administration's negotiating team in Geneva. Amstutz's experience with GATT includes drafting the original U.S. proposal to the Uruguay Round.

The goal of the talks, as agribusiness sees it, is to eliminate what little protection remains for U.S. small- and medium-sized farms. Labelling price supports and subsidies "barriers to trade," they are using the rhetoric of deregulation and free trade to achieve what they failed to attain in Congress: deregulated prices and the eradication of farm subsidies. Price supports are still currently linked to farm production costs, although loosely. Proposals to "decouple" prices from production costs would completely separate prices from production costs. Because international prices for farm commodities are usually lower than even the U.S. mandated price, agribusiness hopes that decoupling will improve export sales.

Also on the agenda of agribusiness is to use GATT to pressure Congress to replace farm subsidies with welfare-type relief. Should Bush Administration negotiators succeed, the federal government will no longer give subsidies to farmers, which will push many farmers out of farming and onto welfare.

Geneva is a long way from the Jensons' living room, where family members eventually decided to sell their farm. In the end, the decision came down to whether Goran's son Ed, the only offspring interested in taking over the farm, was willing to take the risks involved in trying to keep the farm alive. Ed decided that selling now was a safer bet than the chance of loan default and bank foreclosure.

The Jensons did, however, have a choice. If U.S. officials use GATT decisions to push through more policies promoting agribusiness, small and medium farmers in the United States—and around the world—will have even more limited options in years to come. ∎

Dollars & Sense, September 1989

To Make a Tender Chicken

Poultry workers pay the price

By Barbara Goldoftas

In 1983 Donna Bazemore took the best-paying job she could find in northeastern North Carolina—gutting chickens for Perdue Farms. At first she slit open carcasses; later she became a "mirror trimmer" on the night shift. As the birds moved by on the assembly line, a federal inspector next to her examined their far sides in a mirror. He pointed out unacceptable tumors, bruises, and other "physical defects," which Bazemore sliced off with huge scissors.

While the job paid better than the minimum wage she might have earned elsewhere, the conditions were grueling. Bazemore worked in 90-degree heat as the chickens sped by, 72 to 80 a minute. Strict work rules limited bathroom breaks. The primarily black, female work force faced sexual harassment and racism from the white male supervisors. And the women endured a slew of medical problems, ranging from skin rashes to cuts to swollen, painful hands and arms.

Several months after becoming a mirror trimmer, Bazemore noticed that she had no feeling in several fingertips. The numbness progressed to pains shooting up the inside of her arm— symptoms of carpal tunnel syndrome, a potentially disabling disorder caused by overly repetitive movements.

Even after surgery, the trouble continued. "I had no strength in my hands," she says. "I couldn't do the littlest tasks around the house, like sweep a floor or stir for long periods of time. I couldn't write six or seven words without having to rest my hand."

Bazemore is one of thousands of workers hurt by their jobs in poultry processing plants—the polite term for slaughterhouses. "Work in poultry plants by every stretch of the imagination is horrible," says Artemis (her full name). She has worked for two different companies in northern Arkansas, a region thick with poultry plants. "It's stressful, demanding, noisy, dirty. You're around slimy dead bodies all the time. And it's very dangerous."

According to its trade journal, *Broiler Industry,* the industry makes "staggering" profits. Demand for poultry has grown steadily for decades, and U.S. consumers now eat more chicken and turkey than red meat. Production increased by 67% in just 10 years, from 12 billion pounds in 1977 to about 20 billion pounds in 1987.

The industry's growth and profitability have in large part come at the expense of poultry workers who, according to the Bureau of Labor Statistics, suffer twice the average private sector rates of illness and injury. As poultry processing expanded, it grew increasingly concentrated. Firms converted to large-scale assembly-line operations, ultimately speeding up and deskilling individual jobs. The resulting breakneck pace and repetitive motions tax workers' hands and arms—and can ultimately cripple them.

A CHICKEN IN EVERY POT

The poultry industry of 50 years ago hardly resembled the one that ConAgra, Tyson Foods, and Perdue now dominate. Small farmers raised most chickens and turkeys, sending them to private, local slaughterhouses. The birds were smaller and more expensive than those sold today. People ate less poultry and usually bought it whole.

In the 1940s, poultry scientists created new breeds of birds that grew faster and did not waste away in crowded conditions. The innovations made large-scale operations both feasible and efficient. In the 1940s and 1950s, giant "integrators," which already owned slaughterhouses, animal feed mills, and hatcheries, bought out the small chicken farms as well.

Since the 1960s, processing has undergone a similar transformation. Mechanizing parts of their operations enabled firms to increase the volume and size of their plants. The industry also grew more consolidated. In 1977, the top four firms slaughtered just 20% of all chickens killed in the United States. By 1987, their portion had nearly doubled to 38%. During that same period, poultry companies used the gimmick of name-brand poultry to secure a larger share of the retail mar-

BARBARA GOLDOFTAS, a *Dollars & Sense* editorial associate, is a freelance writer.

The resulting breakneck pace and repetitive motions of poultry processing tax workers' hands and arms—and can ultimately cripple them.

Poultry workers organize

Three-fourths of poultry processing happens in Arkansas, Georgia, Alabama, and North Carolina. The warm climate allows year-round production, and the poultry firms also prefer the southern labor climate—cheap and largely unorganized.

For many workers, poultry jobs are steadier and easier than field work. And the companies pay more than convenience stores and fastfood joints, usually between $4.50 and $6.00 an hour.

The price of the job, though, is high—a worker's safety and health—and even in anti-union areas, workers are starting to organize. At the Cargill plant in Buena Vista, Georgia, workers say the Retail, Wholesale, and Department Store Union (RWDSU), which survived a recent decertification drive there, gives them a say about their health.

"A lot of people are afraid to speak up, afraid to get fired," says Felton Toombs, who was fired three months after having carpal tunnel surgery last year. "You need someone to speak up for you when something goes wrong."

In northeastern North Carolina, the Center for Women's Economic Alternatives (CWEA) teaches workers that they should not have to choose between their job and their health. Organizers offer clinics about repetitive motion injuries, and they have helped hundreds of Perdue workers get medical care and workers' compensation. Workers are now asking to be sent to the doctor, says former Perdue worker Bazemore. "A couple months ago, they were losing fingers and arms and they would never complain."

ket. They began selling directly to the fast-food and retail outlets, and they introduced new, expensive products that required further processing.

A typical poultry plant now processes tens of thousands of chickens each day. One by one, live birds are hung by the feet on a moving line of hooks called shackles and mechanically stunned, decapitated, and scalded to remove the feathers. They are quickly gutted and then cut into parts, packaged whole, or sped through a deboning line.

Throughout the plant, workers perform simple, highly repetitive jobs. They draw out guts, pull livers, cut wings and gizzards, pop thigh bones. Most do a single, defined movement—cutting, slicing, lifting birds onto the shackles, or pulling breast meat from the bone with their fingers. They may repeat this motion 25, 40, 90 times a minute, hour after hour. "They treat you as if you were a machine, plugged in, running on electricity," says Rita Eason, another former Perdue worker.

Like Bazemore, many workers do their jobs in conditions of extreme heat or cold. Processing involves both ice and scalding water, and plant temperatures reportedly vary from 26 to 95 degrees. Bazemore's department lacked ventilation, despite the heat, and in other departments, she says, "people wear three, four, five pair of socks and long underwear all year. And they're still cold."

Although the work is fast and hard, the companies allow few scheduled breaks, usually just lunch and two 10- or 15-minute rests each day. At many plants, a strict disciplinary system keeps workers in line—literally. Returning late from a break or missing part of a day, regardless of the reason, brings an "occurrence" or "write-up." After a certain number of write-ups, workers are "terminated."

"If you had to go to the bathroom more than once in two or three hours, they would threaten to write you up," says Brenda Porter, who worked at a Cargill plant in Buena Vista, Georgia, for 12 years.

Afraid to ask permission to leave the line, or forbidden to leave, workers sometimes urinate, vomit, and even miscarry as the chickens pass by. Although it has been nine years since Eason worked at Perdue, she remembers clearly seeing "a grown woman stand on the line and urinate right on herself. She was too scared to move. But then she got so cold she walked out and went home."

A constant risk of illness and injury compounds the harsh day-to-day conditions in the plants. Common ailments include warts, infections from bone splinters, and rashes from the chlorine water used to wash birds contaminated with feces. Workers often lose fingernails and toenails, and they suffer injuries from the knives, saws, and machinery.

The speed and repetition of the work cause the most serious problems. Performing the same action for hours and hours makes poultry workers highly susceptible to debilitating conditions of the nerves, muscles, and tendons. These cumulative trauma disorders, also called repetitive motion injuries, occur among a wide range of workers, from letter sorters to textile workers to typists. According to the Bureau of Labor Statistics, the disorders are the fastest-growing occupational disease of the 1980s.

Carpal tunnel syndrome, which damaged Bazemore's arms, is the most severe such disorder. When the tendons passing though a narrow channel in the wrist—the carpal tunnel—are overused, they swell and press on the nerve that controls feeling in the hand. The result can be painful—and permanently disabling.

Although Mary Smith only worked at Cargill for seven months, her brief stint at the Buena Vista plant left her with hands that hurt day and night. She started in March 1988, trimming bruises and tumors from chicken skin. The pain began in June. "At first they would swell. The nurse said it was normal; I had to get used to the job," she says. "They started hurting real bad and getting numb, especially at night. I'd wake up, shake them, lay them on the pillow. It didn't do no good."

She has not worked since last September but, says Smith, "I still have problems holding things. It hurts to wash dishes, take clothes out of the machine. My arm hurts at night, hurts all day. I get so frustrated sometimes, I feel like just cutting it off." She is hardly alone. At least 14 of her co-workers have had surgery for carpal tunnel syndrome. Union stewards at the plant estimate that more than a third of the workers there have trouble with their hands.

'THEY WEAR OUT'

While gutting and cutting chickens were never easy, poultry work became even harder as the industry expanded. During the 1960s and 1970s, firms increased their productivity by replacing workers with machines. A skilled worker, for example, could slaughter about 66 birds a minute, while a killing machine beheads five times as many—five a second. To meet the recent rise in demand, the plants sped up production, and workers now work at a faster pace for longer hours. Between 1975 and 1985, output per worker increased by 43%.

The U.S. Department of Agriculture (USDA), which regulates slaughterhouses, facilitated the speed-up. Federal inspectors check each bird before and after slaughter, working no faster than the rate set by the agency. Since 1979, USDA engineers have pared down the inspection time allowed for each bird. Upper limits jumped from 57 to 70 birds a minute for two inspectors, even reaching 91 for some high-speed plants.

Safe-food advocates worry about contaminated birds and rising rates of salmonella infections, but the speed-ups have also been critical to the 150,000 workers who process poultry. The changes constituted a "policy shift toward de facto deregulation," says Tom Devine of the Government Accountability Project, a whistleblower support group in Washington, D.C. that has worked with former USDA inspectors. "The idea was to keep the USDA seal of approval but get inspectors out of the way of faster line speeds."

The agency simply determines how quickly inspectors can work "comfortably," says Patrick Burke of the USDA's Food Safety and Inspection Service. "They wear out if the rate's too fast." Asked about how the speed-up might affect other workers, whose "comfort" is not monitored, Burke says that the USDA "can't legally do anything with plant employees."

The new, lucrative products of the 1980s—filleted breasts, poultry patties, chicken nuggets—have made poultry work even more physically demanding. Workers who cut or pull the meat from the bone use quick, repetitive motions that are particularly trying on their wrists and hands. Even Cargill spokesman Greg Lauser acknowledges that the "more in-

Death in a poultry plant

In "To Make a Tender Chicken," author Barbara Goldoftas listed some of the occupational hazards faced by poultry workers: repetitive motion injuries, stress, extreme heat and cold. She did not include fire on her list. But on September 3 of this year, 25 poultry workers in Hamlet, North Carolina, paid the ultimate price for the greed and indifference of the poultry corporations, perishing in a blaze that started in the deep fat fryer at an Imperial Food Products plant. An additional 54 people were injured in the fire.

Witnesses reported that the plant, with 90 people inside, had only one functional door. The company had locked or blocked other doors. The plant lacked automatic sprinklers, had only one fire extinguisher, and no evacuation plan—all violations of workplace codes. The workers "were screaming 'Let me out,'" one passer-by said. "They were beating on the door."

While Imperial's neglect of worker safety is inexcusable, occupational safety and health advocates also fault the laissez-faire attitude of federal and state regulators, and the one-sided pro-business slant of North Carolina's Commerce Department. Mark Schulz, Executive Director of the North Carolina Occupational Safety and Health Project (NCOSH), describes the state of affairs in North Carolina workplaces as "industrial genocide." A worker dies on the job in North Carolina roughly every other day. The state has only 27 safety inspectors and 14 health inspectors to monitor 180,000 workplaces. "Even the state Labor Secretary admits the inspectors can only visit each plant once every 75 years," Schulz points out. No inspector visited the Imperial Food Products plant in Hamlet during its 11 years of operation.

But North Carolina is not alone. "The state of occupational safety and health is so bad in the whole country, it wouldn't surprise me if it happened anywhere," says Schulz. "Federal OSHA [the Occupational Safety and Health Administration] stinks, state OSHA stinks, and workers simply don't have any power." Since the Reagan administration cut OSHA funding and staff in the early 1980s, a string of workplace disasters has occurred: a building collapse in Bridgeport, Connecticut, killed 28 workers; a Pasadena, California, explosion took 23 lives; and 17 died in an accident at Arco Chemical in Channelview, Texas.

The Comprehensive OSHA Reform Act (HR3160, S1622) currently before Congress offers a possibility of ending the bloodshed. The law would mandate joint labor-management safety committees in every workplace of 10 or more and would empower workers to inspect working conditions, receive training on hazards, and shut down unsafe jobs—without having to rely on state or federal inspectors. Schulz says that though pro-business opposition to the Act is strong, outrage from the Imperial Food blaze gives the reform a fighting chance.

To register support for the OSHA Reform Act, call your Representative or Senator, the Senate Labor Committee (202) 224-5375, or House Education and Labor Committee (202) 225-4527. For more information, call the AFL-CIO Dept. of Occupational Safety and Health at (202) 637-5366.

Source: Reprinted from *Dollars & Sense,* November 1991.

tensive processing operations tend to have a greater incidence of repetitive motion injuries."

Many workers suffering from repetitive motion injuries have a hard time getting treatment because of hostile management, untrained nurses, and doctors who know little about their medical problems. "When you tell people you're hurting, they don't really believe you," says Perdue worker Rose Harrell, who was bounced from doctor to doctor before being diagnosed with carpal tunnel. "I told the plant manager that I didn't mind working, but my hands hurt. 'What you telling me for,' he said. 'I can't stop your hands from hurting.'"

Workers and union officials at plants throughout the South describe similar circumstances. "At Cargill [in Buena Vista] when a worker notices her hands are hurting, she'll be given Advil and told that she's just breaking them in," says Jamie Cohen, health and safety director for the Retail, Wholesale, and Department Store Union (RWDSU), which represents the plant's work force. "The previous nurse apparently even told some people, 'Go back and take the pain like the rest.'"

Workers also report being fired after they developed "hand problems." "The procedure is to keep you from going to the doctor instead of sending you to the doctor," says Zelma Ghant, a union steward at the Buena Vista plant who accompanies workers to the nurse. "Instead of facing the problems, the company tries to scare people. When a person is persistent, they find a way to terminate them, to set an example for the rest: If you don't keep quiet, this will happen to you."

Ignoring cumulative trauma disorders can aggravate them, though. Untreated, temporary damage can become permanent, and even a short delay can make a difference. Companies could help limit damage by giving employees less strenuous tasks or letting them rotate jobs. Instead, some workers report being given work that only makes their injuries worse.

Unfortunately, poultry companies have a built-in incentive to ignore injuries—it keeps workers' compensation costs down. Until recently they showed very low rates on their OSHA "200 logs," where they record work-related injuries

and illnesses. The disorders are "underreported," says Roger Stephens, federal OSHA's sole ergonomist, who studies how the design of a workplace affects workers. "The reporting just doesn't go on."

Benny Bishop, plant manager of Southland Poultry in Enterprise, Alabama, says there are "few injuries" to report. "Every injury that has been reported has been recorded," he claims. RWDSU representative Linda Cromer, who worked on a recent union drive there, agrees that the past five years of Southland's OSHA logs show "virtually no repetitive motion injuries listed. But," she adds, "we hear about it on every house call."

a North Carolina attorney who handles compensation cases for injured workers. "People shouldn't have to feel pain every day just to make a living." He says that OSHA historically overlooked the design of assembly-line work, focusing instead on safety standards and a narrow definition of illness and injury.

Companies could make some changes immediately, says Sarah Fields-Davis, director of the Center for Women's Economic Alternatives, a worker advocacy group in Ahoskie, North Carolina. "Redesigning tools and keeping scissors sharp so people don't have to use their backs to cut doesn't cost that much," she says. "Neither does rotating workers" or giving them longer breaks.

The new lucrative products of the 1980s—filleted breasts, poultry patties, chicken nuggets—have made poultry work even more physically demanding.

In a written statement sent to a congressional hearing on cumulative trauma disorders in early June, Perdue Farms claims that "grossly inaccurate media reports have created undue concern" about these disorders. Yet an internal memo from the Perdue personnel department this past February tells a different story. In response to a worker's complaint, it states that it is "normal procedure for about 60% of our work force" at the Robersonville plant to go to the nurse every morning to get pain killers and have their hands wrapped.

Perhaps in an effort to shake its reputation of ineffectualness, OSHA recently levied huge fines against meatpackers and poultry companies for failing to report repetitive motion injuries. But on both the federal and state level, OSHA has been slow to respond to the cause of repetitive motion injuries—the very nature of poultry work.

"I think there will have to be limits on the physical demands employers can make of employees," says Steve Edelstein,

Former Perdue worker Donna Bazemore believes that companies like Perdue should retrain workers disabled by poultry work. After a woman develops carpal tunnel, they should "realize that it's going to be hard for [her] to make a living," she says.

"We're not advocating that Perdue leave," says Fields-Davis. "We just want the company to become more responsive to—and responsible for—the people who are making them rich." ∎

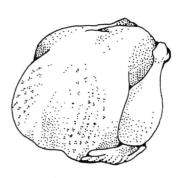

Dollars & Sense, July/August 1987

Rexall for Profits

A drug industry profile

By Jacqueline Orr

You've had a hard day at work, and now you've got a splitting headache. Luckily, your home medicine chest offers plenty of remedies: from Bayer's classic to Tylenol and the generic aspirin substitutes, your choices are endless.

But while the drug products you use to cope with the stress of modern living are many and varied, the companies that make them tend to be large and few. The U.S. pharmaceutical industry today consists of about 1,200 companies that sell everything from prescription medicines to bunion pads and motor oil. Of those, only 16 large firms, including Upjohn, Merck, Eli Lilly, American Home Products, Bristol-Myers, Warner-Lambert, and Smith-Kline-Beckman, control most of the U.S. market.

The large drug firms also stand out in the international arena. Of the top 20 firms worldwide that make up over 70% of all drug sales, 11 are U.S.-based. Total global drug production reached an estimated $128 billion in 1985; of that, $30 billion was produced in the United States.

DRUGS AND MONEY

The fact that the pharmaceutical business is extremely profitable has drawn attention from critics and investors alike. Drug profits regularly run one and a half to two times higher than average profits for all manufacturing firms. Average rates of return for drug companies recorded by the Federal Trade Commission have been 18.1% since 1958, compared with

JACQUELINE ORR is a graduate student in the Social Economy/Social Justice program at Boston College, where she is studying the impact of multinational corporations on women.

11% in all manufacturing. And they're on the rise. Standard and Poor's Industry Surveys projects a 20% increase in profits for 1987, following an 18% jump in 1986.

In response to charges of profiteering, those in the business cite the time, cost, and risk of drug research and development (R&D). From inception to FDA approval, a new drug can take up to ten years to reach the market, and only about one in nine drugs ever makes it that far. For the drug industry, R&D costs alone are very high; only the semiconductor and information processing industries have higher proportionate costs. The cost of bringing a new drug (including R&D and marketing) to the U.S. market can climb as high as $100 million.

But drug representatives neglect to point out that theirs is a highly oligopolistic industry—one limited to a few sellers who can set prices high and still sell their goods. And their sales are further ensured because of minimal overlap among their products. Most pharmaceutical products are meant to treat a particular condition. A successful company tries to make itself one of a few sources for a specific drug, protecting its product with aggressive marketing. By staking out a "sub-market" in this way, pharmaceuticals maintain oligopoly power and reap luxurious profits. Both R&D and marketing require significant initial investment. But once a drug is on the market, its 22-year patent life keeps the road to profits clear of competition from other firms.

Drug companies frequently claim that no single U.S. firm holds more than 8% of the entire U.S. drug market, a low figure compared with other industries like automobiles or steel. But economist Sanjaya Lall estimates that within drug sub-markets, the top four companies usually account for 60% to 90% of sales.

A recent example of the monopoly potential within drug sub-markets is the rapid recovery of faltering Smith-Kline. In 1974, the company ranked 25th among world drug producers. With the discovery and successful international marketing of Tagamet, a new treatment for peptic ulcers, the company burst into 12th position. In 1986, Tagamet became the first prescription drug whose sales topped $1 billion.

Industry spokespersons are eager to explain that high drug prices are caused by the high costs of R&D. For the U.S. industry, these costs run about 15% of total sales (about $4.7 billion in 1986), rising by 15% or so each year. But high R&D costs are key to preserving the industry's oligopoly structure. They present a "natural" barrier to market entry by small, new firms. In fact, the oligopoly structure encourages companies to devote extraordinary resources to R&D precisely because they can charge such high prices if they find a new drug.

But the industry is less eager to mention that marketing costs also play a crucial role in creating and maintaining high prices and high profits. Author Mike Muller, in his encyclopedic critique of the international drug industry, *The Health of Nations,* estimates promotional spending at 20% of sales for most major drug multinationals. That money is spent primarily on advertising, free samples, sponsorship of conferences, research grants, and donations of equipment to physicians. Because no other institution devotes comparable resources to informing M.D.'s about drugs, these companies have a significant influence over the way the medical establishment views particular health conditions and their treatments.

Marketing strategies target doctors, rather than the drug consumers themselves, since about 75% of drug sales are generated by doctors who prescribe the medicines for their patients. A person who is ill needs medication whether it's expensive or not; therefore, the demand for any drug is said to be inelastic—insensitive to changes in price. Furthermore, because physicians make the decision to use the pharmaceutical products regardless of cost (it's usually up to third-party insurers to cover pricey drugs), firms can keep drug prices high.

PHARMACEUTICAL FORAY

Innovation in the business has clearly been crucial to secure profits. In the 1970s, however, fewer and fewer new drugs hit the market. Worse, R&D costs spiraled upward, climbing from $6.5 million (per innovation) in 1962 to $44.7 million in 1980 (figures not adjusted for inflation). By the mid-1970s, the drug industry was desperate for new horizons.

Enter the biotechnology revolution. Initially, biotech firms appeared to threaten the large pharmaceuticals. Small, independent biotech firms sprang up in the late 1970s, pursuing a whole new array of entrepreneurial possibilities: memory and intelligence enhancers, diagnostics and treatments for AIDS, and cancer therapies. But now, even the giddy promise of the biotech revolution looks like it will ultimately provide more capital, not more competition, to the established drug companies.

As independent biotech firms start to create new products they are developing a need for additional finances and expertise for marketing. Large drug companies, capitalizing on that need, are buying up biotech firms. In 1986, Eli Lilly acquired Hybritech; subsequently, Bristol-Myers bought up Genetic Systems. Such acquisitions appear to be the wave of the future. Though some industry members express concern about the ethical quandaries posed by the new technology, overall the industry is embracing biotech as its future lifeblood. Estimated R&D for the biotech industry is now running at $1.4 billion a year.

Similarly, generic firms seemed at first to be a rising threat. Generics that become well-known can erode consumers' loyalty to brand name products. Generic prices can easily undercut the brand names because production is relatively free from R&D costs. The generic drug business looked especially promising be-

cause generics were bolstered by legislation that sped up their FDA approval process and promoted their use by requiring that Medicare patients be administered generic drugs when available. In addition, a record number of drugs (combined sales of $4 billion) whose patents were due to expire in 1986 held a promising future for generics.

Nevertheless, the pharmaceutical industry was able to meet this challenge. The Department of Commerce publication *U.S. Industrial Outlook 1986* sanguinely predicted the long-term prospects on generics: "Small generic companies will merge with larger drug firms. These mergers will allow smaller generic companies to become innovators." Industry leader American Home Products recently entered the generic market by gaining a controlling interest in Quantum Pharmics, Ltd., a small Long Island-based generics firm. Standard and Poor's notes that 75% of the current ge-

"Excellent work, Digby—you've created a fur coat that even the animal rights people can enjoy."

49

neric market consists of "branded generics" put out by large pharmaceutical firms. In the future, large drug companies will most likely control, rather than compete with, their generic younger cousins.

ROUND THE WORLD WITH DRUGS

Since each drug sub-market is small and specific and contains a limited number of buyers, pharmaceuticals must distribute their products as widely as possible to achieve the greatest profits. So from its beginnings, the modern pharmaceutical industry has been a multinational enterprise. Today, U.S. pharmaceuticals are actively expanding throughout western Europe and the Third World. Sales by foreign subsidiaries as a percentage of total sales increased from 29% to 41% between 1970 and 1980. Some industry leaders, including Johnson & Johnson, make up to 50% of their total sales abroad.

For pharmaceuticals, Third World markets are the growth gold mine. In 1984, the Office of Industry Assessment projected that the potential U.S. share of the market in Asia, Latin America, and Africa was four to five times that in western Europe. Third World firms simply can't compete with entering multinationals. Developing countries in Latin America, Asia, and Africa contribute less than 10% to world drug production. According to OECD figures, foreign companies make 80% of the pharmaceuticals sold in Mexico, 65% in the Philippines, and 73% in Brazil. The Interfaith Center on Corporate Responsibility reported that eight transnational companies controlled 80% of the Bangladesh drug market in 1981.

U.S. firms that sell abroad have a variety of reasons for moving their research and manufacturing facilities abroad, as well. First, governments in some developing countries require foreign firms that want to market their products in the host country to also establish facilities there. Secondly, production of drugs (and other goods made by pharmaceutical companies) done inside the country is more effectively marketed because the company can better capitalize on cultural notions of sickness and health. Pharmaceuticals' marketing of infant formula throughout the Third World depended for years on crews of company "milk nurses," local women who visited rural and urban clinics to promote the product among new mothers.

Like other multinationals, pharmaceuticals are drawn to countries whose governments offer financial incentives for relocation, such as reduced taxes on profits and ample opportunities for profit repatriation. Finally, many U.S. firms look abroad in order to bypass the FDA's expensive, time-consuming approval process. A recent relaxation of FDA regulations now allows companies to sell unapproved drugs abroad.

CAN THE GOVERNMENT JUST SAY NO?

These trends in the U.S. drug industry have not moved forward without opposition from consumer lobbyists, grassroots activists, and regulatory agencies. As early as 1988, Congress passed legislation to protect the U.S. public from the industry's untested or unsafe products. The Food, Drug, and Cosmetics Act required all firms to prove a new drug's safety to the FDA before marketing. The act, which also regulates the advertising and labeling of drugs, was passed after two people died from ingesting "elixirs" containing a solvent used in antifreeze. In 1962, Congress amended the Food, Drug, and Cosmetic Act to add a test of "efficacy" to the FDA approval process, and to further regulate marketing.

But the government's role as guardian of public health has always played second string to its role as promoter of industry research and international competitiveness. For instance, government sponsors 20% of drug industry R&D. The U.S. Department of Commerce's 1984 competitive assessment of the industry baldly states, "Today, the pharmaceutical industry depends more than ever on the academic and government biomedical infrastructure of the nation."

The government's alliance with the drug industry has led it to adopt a dangerous hands-off approach to regulation. This spring, Vice President George Bush played a leading role in creating a new category of super-priority drugs that can be sold before they are tested. (Bush's former position as a board director of Eli Lilly makes the alliance particularly insidious.) The FDA already allows the experimental AIDS drug AZT to be distributed and administered—at $10,000 a dose— even though the usual follow-up process isn't yet complete. While it seems that for people with serious conditions the proposal could be the difference between life and death, critics are concerned it could impede clinical testing for more effective treatments. For the industry, the clause ensures big, quick profits for drugs that are still untested and unproven.

Within drug 'submarkets' for particular conditions, the top four companies usually account for 60% to 90% of sales.

The pharmaceutical industry is one place where the market clearly will not provide its own solutions to price gouging and the sale of hazardous drugs. Currently, consumer critics, international public interest organizations, and grassroots activists offer the greatest hope for protection of people's health against the industry's aggressive pursuit of healthy profits. ∎

RESOURCES: "Drugs in the Third World: Can Pharmaceutical Corporations Meet Health Needs?" Interfaith Center on Corporate Responsibility, October 1982; Mike Muller, *The Health of Nations*; Sanjaya Lall, "Medicines and Multinationals: Problems in the Transfer of Technology to the Third World," *Monthly Review*, March 1977; David Tucker, *The World Health Market: The Future of the Pharmaceutical Industry*, 1984.

Dollars & Sense, November 1992

Who Owns the Government?

How government handouts flow to big campaign donors

By Marc Breslow

Editor's Note: This article is based on and includes excerpts from "Bush's Ruling Class," Common Cause Magazine, April-May-June 1992.

Want to deep-six a criminal investigation of your company? Or keep operating your firm while owing the government hundreds of thousands of dollars for labor law violations? Or perhaps you'd like massive quantities of federally-subsidized water in the midst of a drought? No problem. Just give enough political campaign contributions and you are sure to get a favorable hearing.

In 1988, 249 wealthy individuals gave at least $100,000 each to the Bush Presidential campaign—a total of more than $25 million. These contributors, dubbed "Team 100" by the campaign, donated "soft money" in order to evade federal campaign laws, which, among other things, limit individual contributions to a presidential candidate to $1,000 per election.

Soft money is funding received by the state affiliates of the political parties (although the money is often collected nationally), and supposedly used for party-building purposes, not for influencing

MARC BRESLOW is an editor at *Dollars & Sense*.

national elections. But the Federal Election Commission (FEC) claims that it has no jurisdiction over such spending, and does not know what the money is actually used for. "We do not examine the state committees' books unless someone brings a complaint," said Fred Eiland, a spokesperson for the FEC, in an interview with *Dollars & Sense*. Eiland claims that FEC regulations ban him from stating whether any complaints have been filed, unless the FEC has ruled on a particular case—and he knows of no such rulings.

To what extent have Team 100 donors been able to pull strings in the executive branch at the expense of the public? A six-month investigation by *Common Cause Magazine*, published by the citizens' lobby of that name, revealed that Team 100 contributions have ensured access and influence while obtaining:

- pork barrel handouts;
- import-export assistance;
- appointments to ambassadorships and other federal posts; and
- policies favoring Wall Street, oil, real estate, cable television, and other interests.

Direct connections between contributions and political paybacks are inherently difficult to prove. But research based on government records, corporate documents, interviews, and industry and press reports shows a clear pattern of favorable treatment of Team 100 members.

The top givers to Bush's campaign and

the Republican National Committee (RNC) from 1988 through mid-1992 were Lodwrick Cook of Atlantic Richfield (ARCO) and his company ($862,000), Carl Lindner of American Financial Corp. ($845,000), RJR Nabisco and its executives ($808,000), Dwayne Andreas of ethanol giant Archer Daniels Midland ($652,000), and Henry Kravis of the Wall Street firm Kohlberg Kravis Roberts, which owns a controlling share of Nabisco ($505,000).

The largest bloc of contributors, 60 in total, came from the real estate and construction industries, which jointly anteed up $7.9 million. Twenty one members of Team 100 came from manufacturing industries, 20 from oil and gas interests, 63 from Wall Street interests (such as stock brokers and investment bankers), 18 from the food, alcohol, and tobacco industries, and nine from the health and insurance industries.

Seven Team members, hedging their bets, also gave at least $100,000 to Democrat Michael Dukakis' Presidential bid. Such cross-party contributions are additional evidence that much of the money is given to gain political favors. Rather than providing principled support to politicians, donors hope that whichever candidate is elected will be indebted to them.

Common Cause Magazine documented many cases in which Team 100 members have gained major benefits from the Bush administration. Several are summarized below.

NEVER MIND THE DROUGHT

In the water-scarce southwest of the United States, access to water at subsidized rates is of great value to agri-business interests. While such use has high costs for both taxpayers and the environment, Bush has been more concerned with the needs of Team 100 members James Boswell, Howard Leach, and Howard Marguleas. All are involved in agriculture that relies on water from the Central Valley Project, a massive system of dams and reservoirs in southern California. The J.G. Boswell company is the single largest user of water from the Project.

Due to a lengthy drought in the west, in 1991 the Interior Department had cut off agribusiness's water from the Project. But ten days after speaking to Leach at a campaign fundraiser in February 1992, the president unveiled a 326 billion-gallon emergency allocation of Central Valley water for local growers—enough to serve five million urban customers for 18 months.

Three years earlier, in the face of a 960-acre cap on the size of farms eligible for federal low-cost water, Boswell split his 23,000-acre farm into parcels smaller than 960 acres. He then sold them at bargain prices to the Westhaven Trust, which was set up in the name of 326 employees. The ploy worked: Interior ruled that the Trust would be eligible for water at $13 an acre-foot, less than a third the price charged to large farms, at a cost to taxpayers of about $2 million a year.

Interior Secretary Manuel Lujan later conceded Boswell's arrangement was counter to the spirit of the water program, but has let it stand. Helped by the low-cost water, Boswell's California operation is the nation's top cotton producer.

INFLUENCING TRADE

While the Bush administration has been a major promoter of international free trade, it's not above protecting certain industries when Team 100 members are involved. Take the cement industry, which since 1960 has repeatedly tried to block imports from Mexico, Japan, Venezuela and other nations. The industry has filed petitions with the U.S. Commerce Dept. and International Trade Commission claiming that these countries are "dumping" cement at prices below the cost of production. From 1975 to 1988 the federal government rejected five straight petitions, including two during the Reagan Administration.

All that changed when Bush came to office. On September 26, 1989, Southdown, Inc. of Houston led a group of cement manufacturers in asking for protection from Mexican imports. Three days later, Southdown gave the RNC $25,000. Southdown's corporate counsel is Bush $100,000 donor Edgar Marston III.

Within two months the Commerce Department ruled that imports were hurting U.S. manufacturers. By early 1992 the Bush administration had ruled favorably on all three anti-dumping petitions filed by the domestic cement industry, virtually driving out imports from Mexico, Japan, and Venezuela.

HELPING SPECULATORS

Why would 60 real estate business people give $7.9 million to Bush's campaign and the RNC? Not, presumably, out of pure altruism. Among other things, they wanted restoration of the "passive loss" tax shelter. This loophole allows losses on real estate investments to be used as tax deductions, even if the investors are not actively participating in the real estate business. The result is to reduce the federal income taxes owed by investors who have losses in real estate but profits from other industries. The shelter provided a classic write-off: New properties could make money by losing money. Before it was abolished in 1986, this loophole helped spur the speculative commercial overbuilding of the 1980s, by encouraging real estate investment solely to get tax deductions. Such overbuilding in turn helped sink the nation's savings and loan institutions.

In 1991, Treasury Secretary Nicholas Brady and Federal Reserve Chair Alan Greenspan cautioned against reviving this tax break. But in December 1991, representatives of a dozen real estate trade groups met with Bush. Present was Robert Larson, chair of the National Realty Committee, on whose board of directors sit five Team 100 members. Ever ready to respond to his constituents, Bush called on Congress to restore the passive loss tax shelter in his January 1992 State of the Union address.

EXPLOITING WORKERS

Farmworkers' rights advocates blame sugar baron Jose Fanjul's ties to Bush for the Labor Department's failure to crack down on his company's abuse of Caribbean workers. Fanjul's Flo-Sun company dominates the Florida sugar industry, with 160,000 acres and three processing mills. Fanjul also grows sugar cane on a 240,000 acre spread in the Dominican Republic.

Team 100 member Fanjul and his company have given $200,000 in soft money to help elect Bush in 1988 and to the RNC since then. Fanjul was a Bush fundraiser in 1988 and is a finance committee vice-chair for the '92 Bush-Quayle campaign. In 1987 and 1988 the Labor Department fined Fanjul's Okeelanta sugar mill $2.5 million for minimum wage and work rule violations, but settled for 12 cents on the dollar. According to congressional investigators, the Department imposed $267,000 in fines for additional 1988 and 1989 violations, but more than a year passed without Labor collecting the fine. Meanwhile, it allowed Okeelanta to import workers for the 1990 season "without requiring any proof of discontinuation of the unlawful employment practices found in the prior year," notes a congressional report.

MY FAVORITE INDUSTRY

Since President Bush spent his formative years in the oil industry, it's not surprising that he would be sensitive to the industry's desires. But a total of $3.8 million in contributions to his 1988 campaign and to GOP national committees since then couldn't hurt. $862,000 from ARCO alone seems to have created a particularly warm spot in Bush's heart.

When Clean Air Act revisions were being debated in 1989, the White House was expected to support incentives for alternatives to gasoline which are less damaging to the environment—such as methanol, derived from natural gas. But, according to government and industry officials, days before Bush unveiled his clean air plan, executives from ARCO and other major oil concerns met with the president. The executives were worried that methanol would harm the $100 billion a year gasoline business.

Soon afterwards "reformulated gasoline," a version of gas which might be slightly less polluting than the normal product, but is likely to cause much greater air emissions than methanol, became part of the Clean Air Act. Which oil company would benefit most? Arco, which had already begun modifying its refineries and was producing a cleaner-burning gas for older cars.

The rest of the industry, well behind in reformulating gas, didn't appreciate ARCO's role. The American Petroleum Institute waged a $1 million ad campaign pointing out that "no testing has been done to show 'Government Gas' is less polluting, more efficient or affordable."

Bush also took special care of ARCO in his national energy strategy. The cornerstone of his proposal was the opening of Alaska's Arctic National Wildlife Refuge (ANWR) to oil drilling. It just so happens that ARCO is the second-largest oil producer in Alaska, after British Petroleum. In 1990 ARCO netted $700 million from its Alaskan holdings.

As the Senate prepared to vote on ANWR, Bush held sessions in the Oval Office to lobby individual senators. But in the wake of the Exxon Valdez oil spill and with strong opposition from environmentalists, the Senate defeated the measure. The oil industry hasn't given up yet, though—now they're pushing ANWR drilling as a way of creating jobs.

EVASION-PROOF REFORMS NEEDED

Common Cause Magazine's research demonstrates that Team 100 is a particularly blatant exercise in influence-peddling. But the necessities of modern political campaigns, complete with sophisticated ads and expensive television time, force most politicians, from both major political parties, to raise large sums of money.

During the first six months of 1992, the Republican and Democratic parties raised $10 million and $5.2 million, respectively, in soft money. Between January 1991 and June 1992, 20 contributors have given more than $100,000 each to the Democrats. But unlike the Republicans, nine of the Democrats' largest donors were labor unions, including the United Steelworkers ($384,000) and the National Education Association ($208,000). Such funds represent thousands of small contributions from workers, rather than the financial power of business owners.

Attempts at campaign finance reform in recent years, such as the $1,000 limit on individual contributions and the provision of federal matching money for presidential elections, were supposed to reduce the influence of moneyed interests. But each try at reform brings with it new methods of evasion, such as the use of soft money that created President Bush's Team 100. More far-reaching reforms (such as total public financing of campaigns), with fewer loopholes, are needed to help shift the American electoral system from one-dollar-one-vote to one-person-one-vote.

One measure, the Congressional Spending Limit and Election Reform Act of 1992, was passed by both the House and Senate. The bill attempted to close the soft money loophole in congressional races, and placed modest limits on contributions by political action committees (PACs). But it was vetoed by Bush, who objected to the proposed partial public financing of House and Senate campaigns—even though he will get $40 million in tax money for his own race this year. ∎

Resources: "Bush's Ruling Class," April-June 1992, and "Bush and Clinton's Fat Cats," Fall 1992, copyright 1992, *Common Cause Magazine*, Washington, D.C.; *Democracy Watch*, Institute for Alternative Journalism, July 1992.

The fundraising parties

The rich haven't bought only Republicans. The Democrats, who have not held the presidency in 12 years but have controlled Congress during most of the past three decades, deserve their share of blame. Money given through political action committees (PACs) has critically influenced decisions on issues such as the savings and loan (S&L) bailout and health care reform.

Paying off depositors in S&Ls is costing taxpayers hundreds of billions of dollars—more than $1,000 for every person in the country. Congress and the president could have resolved the S&L crisis years before the federal government finally began shutting down troubled thrifts. It didn't happen, largely because Democrats in Congress refused to take action. Michael Waldman of Congress Watch, an organization founded by Ralph Nader, argues the reason is "they were getting money from the same exact places as the Republicans and passing the same policies. As far as S&Ls and banks were concerned, there weren't two parties. There was one party, the fund-raising party."

During the early 1980s, PACs from the industry contributed more than $2 million to the House and Senate Banking Committees. Democrat Fernand St. Germain, the Chairman of the House Committee, got $150,000. The bailout of Charles Keating's Lincoln Savings Bank alone is costing taxpayers more than $2 billion. Keating, who gave $3 million in political contributions, said in an interview with Pheonix station KTVK:

"One question among the many raised in recent weeks had to do with whether my financial support in any way influenced several political figures who took up my cause. I want to say in the most forceful way that I can, I certainly hope so."

Money can also block legislation, such as for changes in health care financing, where progressive reform measures have been stalled in Congress for years. Viveca Novak and Vicki Kemper of *Common Cause Magazine* investigated the health care lobby, finding that there are more than 200 medical industry PACs, which have donated more than $60 million to Congressional candidates in the past decade. Members of the House Ways & Means Committee, through which reform measures are channelled, got an average of $160,000 each from health and insurance industry PACs. Big spenders included the American Medical Association ($12 million), the National Association of Life Underwriters ($6 million), and the American Dental Association ($4 million).

Resources: "Who Owns Our Government," *Listening to America* with Bill Moyers, Public Affairs Television, April 7, 1992.

Dollars & Sense, October 1990

The World Is Their Ashtray

U.S. tobacco companies seek new markets

By Chris Tilly

In Chicago, a middle-class professional calling himself "Mandrake" whitewashes cigarette billboards in the African-American community.

The town of White Bear Lake, Minnesota, bans vending machine sales of cigarettes. Dozens of towns across the country follow suit.

In Philadelphia, an unprecedented coalition of African-American community leaders and public-health advocates forces R.J. Reynolds to cancel test marketing of Uptown, a new cigarette targeted specifically at blacks..

Even Greensboro, North Carolina, in the heart of the nation's top tobacco-producing state, passed a tough ordinance limiting smoking in many public areas.

Politically, U.S. cigarette companies are on the defensive. But financially, these corporate giants are on the attack. In response to the anti-smoking movement, they have diversified their holdings to include non-tobacco-related products. They have fine-tuned their marketing strategies, including developing new brands aimed primarily at narrower market niches—particularly women, young people, and people of color. Most important to their future, these companies have continued to invade and develop new markets in the Third World, where

CHRIS TILLY, a member of the Dollars & Sense Collective, teaches urban planning at the University of Lowell.

regulation is often limited and education about the dangers of smoking is virtually nonexistent.

THE BIG SIX

Six companies control the U.S. cigarette industry with sales in 1985 that totaled $30.2 billion and profits that surpassed $6 billion. The two largest companies, Philip Morris (Marlboro, Merit, Virginia Slims) and R.J. Reynolds (Winston, Camel, Salem), have cornered 70% of the U.S. market. The remaining four—Brown & Williamson (Kool, Viceroy), The American Tobacco Co. (Lucky Strike, Carlton), Lorillard (Newport, Kent, True), and Liggett & Myers Tobacco Co. (Eve, L&M, Lark) divide up the rest of the market. All six trace their lineage to The American Tobacco Company, a multinational empire founded by James "Buck" Duke in the 1890s, modeled on Standard Oil, and split up by trust-busters in 1911.

As these tobacco giants have found, manufacturing cigarettes is extremely profitable. They enjoy what Salomon Brothers stock analyst Diana Temple calls a "peaceful competitive structure," competing with advertising images rather than undercutting each other's prices. With anti-smoking temperament riding high and the cost of launching new brands prohibitive, the tobacco cartel hardly needs to worry about new competition at home. Furthermore, nicotine's addictive properties give cigarette makers a virtually captive market. Recent research by University of Chicago econo-

mist Gary Becker and others shows that when cigarette prices go up by 10%, the amount of cigarettes sold falls by only 7.5%. Simple arithmetic shows that the Big Six can profit from price increases.

But since the early 1950s, when the studies first linked cigarettes to lung cancer, the Big Six have faced one complication: Cigarettes kill people. In fact, smoking tobacco kills close to 400,000 people a year in the United States—more deaths than from AIDS, illicit drugs, murders, suicides, and car accidents combined. Worldwide, tobacco kills an estimated 2.5 million people. New evidence on the toll of passive, "sidestream" smoking may boost these figures considerably: One estimate of U.S. deaths from passive smoking put the total at 46,000 per year.

Since 1964, when Surgeon General Luther Terry released a highly publicized report detailing the health hazards of smoking, the companies' problem has been particularly acute. More recently, health officials, insurance companies, and anti-smoking activists have intensified campaigns to restrict the sale and use of cigarettes, and the percentage of U.S. adults who smoke has fallen from almost one-half the population to less than one-third. Each year in the United States, the number of smokers falls by around 2%.

The tobacco companies have responded in part by diversifying. All six are now multi-product conglomerates, selling everything from Miller Beer (Philip Morris) to Oreos (RJR/Nabisco) to life insurance (American Brands).

But does this mean they've decided to eventually quit the tobacco habit? "That would be like persuading the Medellin cartel to get out of drugs," comments Phillip Wilbur, director of the Smoking Control Advocacy Resource Center, a Washington, D.C.-based anti-smoking information clearing-house. Three-quarters of Philip Morris's profits, and almost two-thirds of RJR/Nabisco's, still come from tobacco. As Fortune magazine put it, "Only the mint makes money more easily."

Instead, the companies use the business clout gained from diversifying to sell more cigarettes and stop the anti-smoking campaign. For example, when R.J. Reynolds bought Nabisco, it acquired an international marketing network, which it has since put to use. And the tobacco conglomerates have used the threat of pulling non-cigarette as well as cigarette advertising to discourage the media from presenting anti-smoking information. RJR Nabisco pulled its advertising account from the Saatchi & Saatchi agency after the firm did an ad campaign for Northwest Airlines on a new smoke-free flight policy.

THEY'VE COME A LONG WAY, BABY

Rather than get out of the business, the tobacco firms are seeking new ways to expand markets. That means competing for those who already smoke and hooking new smokers to replace the 1.3 million who quit and the thousands who die each year. Since male, older, more-educated, and white consumers are quitting smoking most rapidly, the cigarette manufacturers are focusing their sales efforts on young people, women, the less-educated, and people of color.

The companies' main tool is advertising, to the tune of $3.2 billion per year

Since the early 1950s, when studies first linked cigarettes to lung cancer, the Big Six have faced one complication: Cigarettes kill people.

(and counting). Tobacco industry officials publicly maintain that these advertising billions serve only to fight for market share, not to attract new smokers.

"This is utter and complete nonsense," says Emerson Foote, former chairman of the board of McCann-Erickson—an ad agency once responsible for $20 million in cigarette accounts. "I am always amused by the suggestion that advertising, a function that has been shown to increase consumption of almost every other product, somehow miracu-

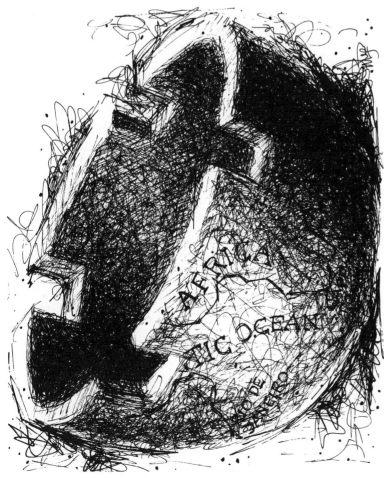

ILLUSTRATION BY MARGARET FAULK

lously fails to work for tobacco products."

A Brown & Williamson marketing executive is more blunt. "Nobody is stupid enough to put it in writing," he says, "but there is always the presumption that your marketing approach should contain some element of market expansion, and market expansion in this industry means two things: kids and women."

Particularly insidious are promotions aimed at teen-agers. Cigarette manufacturers know that since 80% of smokers start by age 18, and 90% by age 21, it's crucial to entice new customers early. The companies' public line is to deplore sales of cigarettes to minors (which account for $221 million in profits yearly) and to deny aiming advertising at teens. But the companies' private dollars buy ad campaigns that use youthful models and saturate advertising in magazines with large teen-aged readerships.

Saturation advertising is just one part of the cigarette companies' overall promotional scheme of market segmentation—appealing with new brands and targeted advertising to a specific group of current or potential smokers. The tobacco industry figured out decades ago that by introducing a new brand that appealed directly to women they could sell more cigarettes. Since then Virginia Slims, More, Eve, and Satin have hit the market. The companies have continued to segment the market to narrower niches. From only 18 brands of cigarettes in 1950, the number has grown to over 50 brands with 200 styles. Market segmentation has reached such levels of cynicism that RJR pitched its new Dakota brand to what the ad agency confidentially called "Virile Females"—tough, less-educated, working-class girls and women (see box).

Cigarette manufacturers have also directed their sights at people of color. "The overall [tobacco] market is tending toward downscale and low-economic consumers," commented a former tobacco executive anonymously. "And that often means blacks and Hispanics." RJR's disastrous attempt to market Uptown to blacks is the most famous example, but Uptown is only the latest in a long line of marketing calculations. The main menthol brands (Kool, Salem, Newport) are marketed primarily to blacks. In addition to magazine advertising ($3.3 million per year in Ebony alone), the companies lean heavily on the "eight-sheet billboard"—small, five-foot by eleven-foot billboards close to street level, where children, among others, are likely to see them. In 1985, tobacco companies spent $5.8 million on these billboards in black communities—over one-third of total advertising by all advertisers in this medium. Recently-launched brands aimed at Latinos include Dorado, Rio, and L&M Superior.

As the anti-smoking chorus grows louder, the tobacco companies are also busy devising new ways to quiet the drum beat and continue to sell cigarettes. A new wave of products takes aim at the passive smoking issue. Philip Morris's Superslims and RJR's Excel are sold as "low-smoke" cigarettes. Their secret: Additives that render the smoke less visible, without actually reducing its amount. In fact, chemists at the American Health Foundation found Excel's sidestream smoke has higher concentrations of certain toxic compounds than traditional cigarettes. RJR also has inaugurated a perfumed cigarette, Horizon, with scratch-and-sniff patches in magazines.

THE SMOKING VISE

Ultimately, with the U.S. anti-smoking campaign growing, the market here is limited: The future for the Big Six lies in the Third World. While the number of smokers has slowly declined in most developed countries, it has grown by about 3% per year in developing countries. China's smokers alone consume 1.4 trillion of the world's five trillion cigarettes yearly. In 1987, U.S. cigarette exports totaled $2.6 billion, less than one-tenth of total sales but more than double the amount of export sales three years earlier.

In the Third World, the cigarette com-

Segmenting the market: Uptown and Dakota

Earlier this year, R.J. Reynolds hoped to rectify some of its marketing weaknesses by introducing two new cigarette brands—Uptown and Dakota. As the *Wall Street Journal* explained, RJR's flagship brands, Winston and Camel, "have suffered from not being sufficiently targeted to specific-enough audiences."

Uptown was to be marketed explicitly to urban African-Americans. RJR sheathed these menthol cigarettes in slick black and gold packaging, featured African-American models, and even placed the cigarettes in the pack filter-side down after market researchers told them that many blacks open cigarette packs from the bottom.

When word of a planned test-marketing of Uptown in their community reached Philadelphia's African-American leaders, RJR met with stiff resistance. The local National Association for the Advancement of Colored People (NAACP), the Urban League, and black U.S. Health and Human Services secretary Louis Sullivan joined forces with ministers, educators, civic groups, and public health advocates to denounce Uptown.

As pressure mounted, RJR canceled the test marketing but refused to say whether they would drop the product altogether.

Meanwhile, RJR was still working on another promotional effort, code-named Project VF (Virile Female), to create a new "Dakota" brand targeted to blue-collar women. Women under 23 are the fastest-growing group of smokers in the nation, but their most popular brand is Marlboro, produced by RJR's chief rival, Philip Morris.

As of early 1990, RJR had already spent $1.3 million on these plans. Below is part of RJR's confidential Dakota target market profile that the Women vs. Smoking Network obtained:

- Age/gender: Caucasian females, age 18-20 (secondarily 21-24).
- Education: No education beyond high school.
- Occupation: Entry level service or factory job.
- How she spends her free time: With her boyfriend doing whatever he is doing.
- Events they attend: Drag races, motorcross, hot rod shows, tractor pulls, wrestling.

Proposed promotions include "Star in a Romance Novel" sweepstakes and "Night of the Living Hunks," with male strip shows in selected bars. The company would introduce a heavy metal band, also named Dakota, with the same "look" as the cigarette brand. The band would be featured in "video kiosks" in bars and clubs (narrowly skirting the TV advertising ban enacted in 1970).

RJR planned a test market for April 1990 in Houston. When Women vs. Smoking and others challenged the Dakota sales pitch, RJR postponed the test. Unlike the case of Uptown, however, RJR has publicly continued to develop Dakota, claiming that it has altered its marketing plans from the ones that got leaked, despite the fact that the company is using ads virtually identical to those in the original marketing plans.

GHETTO BILLBOARDS WE NEVER GOT TO SEE:

Some say "ballot" & some say "bullet" but everybody says "UPTOWN"

WARNING: The Surgeon General has determined that smoking will kill you

NICK THORKELSON

panies see a growing market without the restrictive regulation and increasing health education they face at home. For example, only 24% of developing countries require warning labels on cigarettes, compared to 95% of industrial nations.

But first the Big Six had to get past the trade barriers many nations had established against tobacco imports. With North Carolina Senator Jesse Helms as their point man, they've convinced the U.S. government to press Asian countries to drop the barriers by threatening retaliatory trade measures.

The example of Taiwan is instructive. Until 1987, the government had a tobacco monopoly, stiff restrictions and tariffs on imported brands, and an ad ban on both domestic and imported cigarettes. But the government of Taiwan caved in to U.S. pressure, ending both the trade restrictions and the ad ban. Tobacco salespeople from U.S. companies rushed into the country to begin promotions, targeting teen-agers. They distributed free cigarettes at disco parties, advertised heavily in youth magazines, and offered free tickets to a concert by a Taiwanese pop star in return for five empty cigarette packages.

The results were dramatic. Between 1986 and 1987 Taiwan's tobacco imports jumped elevenfold. The Taiwanese smoked an average of 80 more cigarettes per person, and teen smoking more than doubled, from 15% of teens to 33%. Demonstrating the effectiveness of U.S. companies' youth blitz, a 1987 survey of 1,005 young smokers in Taipei fast food restaurants found that a stunning four out of five preferred foreign over native cigarettes.

Similar changes in smoking patterns occurred in other countries that lowered barriers against U.S. cigarettes. Japan dropped cigarette import restrictions in 1986 and has become the U.S. companies' largest export market. South Korea followed suit in 1988. The pressure is currently on Thailand.

Latin America and Africa are also targeted export markets. Philip Morris has donated street signs to some South American cities that say "Marlboro" along with the street name. British American Tobacco (BAT), the world's largest tobacco company and owner of U.S.-based Brown & Williamson, has hatched a scheme for expanding sales in Uganda, having seen sales in neighboring Kenya double in five years. Their recipe: High-nicotine cigarettes, no warning labels, and a price Africans can afford—about 12 cents per pack of 20.

THE "ANTIS"

Both in the Third World and back home in the United States, people are increasingly resisting cigarette manufacturers' assaults. In June 1990 Brazil enacted a law banning daytime TV advertising of cigarettes, requiring larger warning labels on packaging and advertising, banning free samples, outlawing smoking in healthcare institutions, and giving the minister of health the authority to suspend the sale of brands that violate the law. In most respects, the law is tougher than anything the United States has enacted.

In the United States, anti-smoking activists (whom Philip Morris, in its *Smokers Advocate* newsletter, simply calls "antis") have pursued a range of strategies. Liberal legislators such as Senator Edward Kennedy (D-Mass.) and Rep. Henry Waxman (D-Cal.) have proposed various cigarette advertising bans. Ad bans are gaining support in the United States as evidence from the Scandinavian countries and Canada has shown that ad restrictions reduce smoking, especially among young people.

Local, state, and national laws mandating smoke-free areas have proliferated. The Tobacco Divestment Project launched in mid-1990, hopes to build tobacco stock divestment decisions by Harvard University and the City University of New York, stimulating a divestment movement along the same lines as the anti-apartheid movement's activities. Another threat to the cigarette companies comes from liability suits by smokers or their surviving relatives, of which 53 are currently pending in the courts. So far, however, plaintiffs have lost all suits against the tobacco industry (except for one 1988 victory later thrown out on appeal.).

Despite these challenges, the political and economic clout of the Big Six remains formidable. Queried by a journalist about whether cigarette manufacturers would eventually get out of the business due to anti-smoking pressures, Tobacco Institute (TI) vice-president William Kloepfer responded with a smile, "I've heard what you've just said since my first day with the TI 20 years ago. Business profits have increased steadily during that time."

Which explains why people like Mandrake have turned to defacing billboards. As Mandrake says, "Direct action is the way to go when you are fighting powerful foes." ■

Labor Markets and Discrimination

Dollars & Sense, March 1990

Trapped on a Pedestal

Asian Americans confront model-minority stereotype

By Thea Lee

"Visit Chinatown U.S.A. and you find an important racial minority pulling itself up from hardship and discrimination to become a model of self-respect and achievement in today's America. At a time when it is being proposed that hundreds of billions be spent to uplift Negroes and other minorities, the nation's 300,000 Chinese-Americans are moving ahead on their own—with no help from anyone else."

—U.S. News and World Report,
December 26, 1966

"Asian Americans are our exemplar of hope and inspiration."

—Ronald Reagan,
as quoted in the *New Republic*, 1985

THEA LEE is a *Dollars & Sense* editor. Her great-great-grandfather came to the United States from China in 1850 to work on the railroad.

In the mid-1960s, when relaxed restrictions dramatically increased Asian immigration to the United States, the popular press, politicians, and others assigned Asian Americans the role of "model minority." When the 1980 Census revealed that median family income for Asian-Americans actually surpassed that of whites by almost 13%, the stories resurfaced with renewed intensity. *Fortune* ran an article entitled, "Superminority" and the *New Republic* chimed in with "America's Greatest Success Story."

The model-minority label, enviable though it might seem, has served Asian Americans badly. It obscures real differences among Asian Americans and exacerbates the resentment of other minority groups. The stories of spectacular achievement are presented as proof that Asian Americans either do not face or have overcome adverse racial discrimination. This not only denies Asian Americans legal and social protection against discrimination, but creates a backlash of its own—as majority or other minority groups lobby to offset their perceived advantage.

PLUS ÇA CHANGE...

Although the nation's 6.5 million Asian Americans still make up less than 3% of the total U.S. population, they are the fastest-growing minority group in the country. According to current estimates, the ethnic Asian population in the United States doubled between 1980 and 1990, as it did between 1970 and 1980. The rapid growth brings with it equally dramatic changes in its composition, rendering the old stereotypes ever more obsolete.

Filipinos recently overtook the Chinese to become the largest single Asian group in the United States (see table). The Japanese-American population remained relatively stable in the 1980s, while the number of Indochinese more than tripled. The number of Asian Indians and Koreans continued to grow at a high rate, with each of those groups constituting a little over 10% of the Asian-American population.

Judged by standard measures of success, the achievements of Asian Americans—as a group—seem impressive. Their median family income in 1979 was $23,100, compared to the national median of $19,900. Moreover, a 1988 study by the Civil Rights Commission found that the hourly wages of most American-born Asian men exceed those of whites with comparable levels of education and experience. According to the 1980 Census, 34% of Asian Americans completed four or more years of college, compared to only 16% of the total U.S. population. And at elite universities, Asian Americans are even more disproportionately represented: in 1986, Asian Americans made up 12% of the freshman class at Harvard, 22% at MIT, and 27% at the University of California at Berkeley.

However, the economic and social reality of Asian immigrants is far more complex than these statistics indicate. Focusing on averages and success stories misses an equally striking case of Asian "over-representation": at the bottom of the barrel. Although Asian Americans are three to five times as likely as whites to be engineers and doctors, they are also two to four times as likely to work in food services or textiles. Many of the poorest Asian Americans are undocumented or paid under the table at sweatshops or restaurants; their incomes are likely to be under-represented by official figures. And offsetting their high educational attainment as a group is the fact that 6% of Asian Americans have not completed elementary school—three times the rate for whites.

To a large extent, deep differences among Asians from different countries, between recent immigrants and longtime residents, and between refugees and skilled professionals swamp the similarities, rendering generalizations misleading. For example, the median income of a Laotian family in 1979 was $5,000, compared to $27,400 for a Japanese family and $25,000 for an Indian family.

The stereotype of the successful minority hurts those Asian Americans who need the most help, because the success of some is used as an excuse to deny benefits to all. The most striking example is in college admissions. Most schools no longer consider Asians a "disadvantaged minority," excluding them from special consideration in the admissions process and in the awarding of financial aid. Some schools have gone a step further and rigged their admissions standards to handicap Asian students. Patrick Hayashi, now the vice-chancellor in charge of admissions at Berkeley, testified that in the mid-1980s, people "seemed to be deliberately searching for a standard which could be used to exclude Asian immigrant applications."

THE AMERICAN DREAM?

Inappropriate and sometimes irrelevant comparisons contribute to racial tension between Asian Americans and other minorities. Black conservative Thomas Sowell, among others, has suggested that blacks would do well to follow the example of Asian Americans—work hard, get a good education, and achieve the American dream.

But American blacks face barriers quite different from those faced by Asian immigrants. Although both black Americans and early Asian immigrants endured legal and personal discrimination during their history in this country, Asian Americans at least came voluntarily. Furthermore, the 1965-75 wave of Asian immigrants consisted largely of highly educated, financially solvent professionals.

Another advantage of some Asian immigrant groups is that they have developed alternative ways to raise capital, ways that depend more on informal financial arrangements among families and acquaintances than on commercial banks. One such method is the rotating credit association.

Called *hui* in Chinese, *kye* in Korean, and *tanomoshi* in Japanese, these self-financing pools originated centuries ago to help families finance major expenses like weddings and funerals. The pools serve an important need once immigrants come to the United States, providing start-up capital to people who might be denied loans by conventional banks for lack of collateral or a poor credit rating. Up to 40 people participate, each contributing savings to a pool, which is loaned out to each participant in turn.

Should blacks, Latinos, and native Americans take a clue from Asian Americans, and set up similar institutions in their communities? That would be one way of dealing with the inadequate and racially discriminatory lending policies of U.S. financial institutions. But the path is a risky one, due to its very informality: If the leader is dishonest, or if one member cannot pay her or his share, the other members can lose their entire investment. As the Wall Street Journal points out, "There is no deposit insurance covering these freewheeling banks, only the integrity of the leader, and stories about crooked operators and defaulted contributions abound in Asian communities."

Moreover, rather than urging other minorities to emulate the circuitous path Asian Americans have taken, policy-makers should work to lift the barriers in the U.S. economy—particularly in the financial system—facing all people of color and recent immigrants. Setting up one minority as the "good minority" and another as "bad" misses the point entirely. Both

Ethnic Asians in the United States
(in thousands)

	1980	1990*	2000*
Japanese	715	800	860
Chinese	810	1,260	1,680
Indian	385	680	1,000
Korean	355	820	1,320
Philippine	780	1,400	2,080
Vietnamese	245	860	1,580
Laotian	55	260	500
Cambodian	15	180	380
All Asians	**3,465**	**6,550**	**9,850**

*Projection
Source: *Pacific Bridges*, ed. Fawcett and Carino.

blacks and Asian Americans suffer from discrimination, albeit different kinds, and both have needs that are unmet by the U.S. economy and current policy.

DISCRIMINATION AND SUCCESS

At face value, the 1980 Census seemed to prove conclusively that Asian Americans

whether discrimination had occurred.

U.S.-born Japanese-American and Korean-American men were found to earn somewhat more annually than comparable non-Hispanic white men. Other Asian groups, however, fared less well. Measured annually, U.S.-born Chinese men earned 5% less, Filipino men earned 9%

The most successful Asian Americans—those held up as examples of super-achievement—are routinely paid less and promoted less often than comparable whites.

---

no longer face discrimination in U.S. labor markets. If they earn more than whites, the argument went, then if anything they must enjoy a relatively advantageous position.

But upon closer scrutiny the Asian income figures reveal a more complex picture, even beyond the differences among nationalities. For one thing, the Asian income advantage evaporates when per capita incomes, rather than median family incomes, are compared. Since Asian-American families tend to be larger than average, with more workers per household, per capita Asian income in 1979 was actually slightly lower than the U.S. average.

But lower income in itself is not proof of discrimination, any more than higher income is proof of its absence. Other factors such as education, experience, and number of years in this country also need to be taken into account. A 1988 report by the U.S. Civil Rights Commission used 1980 Census data to compare annual income and hourly wages for Asian Americans in the six largest national groups: Chinese, Japanese, Filipino, Korean, Indian, and Vietnamese. Adjusting for levels of education, work experience, and geographic location, they tried to isolate race in order to see

less, and Indian men earned 30% less than similarly qualified white men.

Asian women, both immigrants and U.S.-born, earn as much as or more than white women with similar characteristics, although they still earn substantially less than Asian or white men. The earnings gap between black and white women is also significantly smaller than the earnings gap between black and white men. This may occur because women tend to be clustered in lower-paying jobs than men.

Contrary to the stereotype, Asian men as a group work fewer hours per year than white men, although foreign-born Asian men tend to work longer hours than foreign-born white men. The Civil Rights Commission notes that the lower average hours of work "may reflect barriers to employment," such as seasonal or irregular work. Asian-American women, on the other hand, work more hours and weeks per year than white women and are more likely to be in the labor force.

TROUBLE AT THE TOP

Lumping Asian Americans together obscures the fact that within occupations and in some regions of the country, Asian Americans are clearly discriminated against. The most successful Asian

Americans—those held up as examples of super-achievement—are routinely paid less and promoted less often than comparable whites. This effect grows as they climb higher, both in academia and in corporations.

U.S.-born Asian men are less likely to hold managerial positions than whites with comparable skills and characteristics. While Asian Americans make up 4.3% of professionals, they are only 1.4% of officials and managers. The stereotype of Asians as passive and technically oriented may impede their promotion to top managerial positions.

Even though Asian Americans are famous—or infamous?—for their relatively high investment in higher education, both as families and as individuals, they tend to receive a lower return on their education than whites. A study by Jayjia Hsia using 1980 Census data found that Asian-American faculty with stronger than average academic credentials and more scholarly publications were paid less than average. In sum, the labor-market position of Asian Americans—even those at the top—is hardly enviable. They invest heavily in education, only to catch up to whites who have invested somewhat less. They work for corporations, only to find that their bosses have already decided how far they can advance.

ONE WAY OUT

One way that Asian Americans have coped with limited upward mobility and relatively lower access to skilled union jobs has been to buy small businesses. Asian Americans have a high rate of business ownership compared to other minority groups—54.8 business owners for every 1,000 Asians or Pacific Islanders, compared to 12.5 for blacks and 17 for Latinos. The Korean, Chinese, and Japanese business rates are higher than that for all Americans (64 per 1,000).

Although they have provided some opportunities for recent immigrants, small businesses are notoriously difficult to run. A Los Angeles-based study showed that Korean-American-owned enterprises in that city are heavily concentrated in two labor-intensive and highly competitive industries: retail and selected services. These businesses are small, both in terms of the number of employees and the value of sales. Four-fifths of these firms hire five or fewer employees, and nine-tenths hire ten or fewer. Virtually all had sales under one million dollars. Typical of Asian-owned businesses in the rest of the country, their geographic locations are usually outside mainstream markets, in mostly minority communities with high crime and poverty rates. Like all small businesses, they are particularly vulnerable to business cycles, with a higher than average failure rate.

The visibility and the "foreignness" of Asian merchants in the inner cities make them easy targets for resentment. Edna Bonacich, a sociologist at the University of California at Riverside, points out that merchants of any race, by definition, make their livings by making a profit from their customers. Since many of these merchants live elsewhere, she argues, they also tend to reinvest their profits elsewhere. And since many of these Asian-owned businesses employ family members, they offer relatively few jobs to the community.

Bonacich argues that the Asian merchants act as "minority middlemen," and are themselves exploited by the corporations whose goods they sell. It isn't profitable for large chain supermarkets or department stores to sell in inner-city neighborhoods, so Asian immigrants fill the void. Their willingness to face the personal and financial risks involved in operating a business in high-crime areas allows large corporations a bigger market for their goods.

In recent years, black leaders in Harlem, Bedford-Stuyvesant, and elsewhere have led boycotts and protests against Asian merchants in their communities. This anger is misdirected. Asian immigrants buy stores in poor neighborhoods not to take advantage of residents, but because they can't afford the higher rents in more affluent neighborhoods.

WHO'S THE ENEMY?

Many Asian Americans, especially those whose grandparents or great-grandparents came to this country in the late nineteenth or early twentieth century, regard the glowing praise heaped upon the new "model minority" with some skepticism and irony. They may be the new darlings of the media, but for most of the earlier part of this century, Asian

Americans were despised, feared, and legally excluded from many rights other Americans—black and white—took for granted.

In 1870, foreign-born Asians were singled out as the only racial group not eligible for U.S. citizenship. In 1882, the Chinese Exclusion Act virtually barred Chinese from immigrating to the United States. Additional laws passed in the early 1900s extended the ban to Japanese, Koreans, and Filipinos. In many states, Asian Americans could not legally own land or marry whites until after World War II.

In 1965, the U.S. government removed the last vestiges of anti-Asian discrimination from its immigration laws. Today, Asian Americans struggle more with stereotypes and ignorance than with

legal discrimination. Confusion between Asian countries and people of Asian ancestry living in this country can lead to anger and sometimes violence from people frustrated over the outcome of the Vietnam war, the loss of U.S. jobs to Japanese firms, the increasing Japanese ownership of U.S. assets, or even the U.S. trade deficit with Japan.

This confusion cost 110,000 Japanese-Americans their homes, jobs, and freedom during World War II, when the war against Japan spilled over into a war against Japanese-American citizens. In 1982, the same confusion cost Vincent Chin, a Chinese-American man from Detroit, his life when he was beaten to death with a baseball bat by two men reportedly angered by the Japanese success in automobile markets.

Such incidents share roots in economic frustration. Given the current

structure of the U.S. and world economies, there really aren't enough jobs, housing, and resources for everyone, especially in poor neighborhoods. In the short run, it is easier for politicians to take sledgehammers to Japanese-built consumer goods than it is to improve the U.S. position in the world economy. It is easier for conservative economists or sociologists to compare blacks unfavorably to Asian Americans than it is to look at ways in which both face discrimination in U.S. labor markets. But it is important that progressives and organizers in minority and working-class communities resist these same quick-fix solutions.

Less Japan-bashing and more frequent acknowledgement of existing discrimination are a necessary first step to a more realistic assessment of the difficult and

The portrayal of Asian Americans as a superminority not only dehumanizes Asian Americans, it also creates unreasonable expectations.

sometimes tenuous position of new immigrants and non-white Americans. The portrayal of Asian Americans as a superminority not only dehumanizes Asian Americans, it also creates unreasonable expectations (much as the supermom image does). And setting up one minority group against others inevitably creates inter-racial tensions, and sometimes violence. To the extent that blacks and Asians are squabbling over who gets to own ghetto grocery stores, neither is asking why conventional banks aren't lending to either one of them. ■

RESOURCES: Jayjia Hsia, *Asian Americans in Higher Education and at Work,* 1988; U.S. Commission on Civil Rights, *The Economic Status of Americans of Asian Descent: An Exploratory Investigation,* October 1988; *Minority Trendsletter,* Winter 1987.

Dollars & Sense, January/February 1993

Closing the Pay Gap

Women gain on men, but not equally

By Elaine McCrate

I n the 1970s, women activists wore "59 cents" buttons to let people know that women working full-time earned only 59% as much as men, the same as in 1960. Well now it's time to trade in those old buttons—the new ones should read "70 cents." Women in their late 20s have done even better, earning about 85% as much as their male counterparts.

The news is welcome, but puzzling: Why did the pay gap begin to close suddenly in the 1980s, a decade of unremitting hostility from the federal government toward employment opportunity and affirmative action?

Economists have offered three main explanations for the shrinking of the pay gap:
- Women have been accumulating more work experience.
- They have been seeking more formal education.
- Deindustrialization has seriously depressed male wages.

These explanations provide a useful starting point for understanding changes in the gender pay gap, but they also obscure some important differences among women. The focus on average pay hides considerable variation in women's fortunes by race, age, schooling, and family situation. In fact, increasing inequality within each gender accompanied growing overall equality between men and women. For example, black women's pay

ELAINE McCRATE teaches economics at the University of Vermont.

fell from 94% to 89% of white women's between 1977 and 1990.

In short, as we examine the impact of experience, education, and deindustrialization on women's earnings, we need to remember that the pay gap shrank for different reasons for different women.

ON THE JOB

Over the past 10 to 15 years, many women have been spending more time in the wage labor force, and less time on housework and care for their families. In some occupations, more continuous experience helps women climb job ladders. They receive more raises and promotions and build up a list of clients. Recent job experience also means that a woman probably has in place most of the prerequisites for work outside the home: references, transportation, child care, and a set of clothes that can pass muster in an office. Not too long ago, most white women would stay out of the labor force for extended periods, and face putting all these pieces together from scratch when they reentered the work force. They would then have to start jobs at entry-level salaries, well behind men who had been working continuously for years.

Women are entering the labor force out of choice, necessity, or both. Families have fewer children today than in the 1970s, making it easier for women to work outside the home. Women sometimes defer motherhood altogether until their thirties, taking advantage of new educational and career opportunities. A significant number of women also receive more assistance from husbands with

housework and child care than in the 1970s, making it easier to stay in the labor force. Other more prosperous women increasingly count on maids or child care workers to do much of the family work.

In addition, married women put more time into their jobs because they must help compensate for their husbands' stagnant or falling incomes. They may also recognize the economic threat posed to them by a 50% divorce rate, coupled with the sub-poverty level support for unmarried mothers through Aid to Families with Dependent Children (AFDC).

Job experience also explains part of the growing inequality among women. For example, young white women now log more weeks on the job than young black women, the reverse of a long-standing historical distinction between them. This happened for two reasons: Young white women have spent less time at home and more on the job, while young black women, especially those in central cities, have faced a collapse of job opportunities.

AT SCHOOL

In the 1980s, young female job-seekers dramatically upgraded their educational qualifications relative to men. Women now earn a slight majority of the bachelor's degrees awarded each year, and their share of the advanced degrees (master, doctoral, and professional) rose from 38% in 1975 to 47% in 1990. More of these women studied technical subjects, allowing them to break longstanding barriers to lucrative male occupations. Many became architects, lawyers, doctors, and managers. For example, in 1970 only 4% of MBAs were awarded to women; by 1990, a third were. As a result, the percentage of all women workers employed in managerial jobs more than doubled between 1975 and 1990. Overall, the real earnings of young college-educated women increased 20% between the late 1970s and mid-1980s, while those of their male counterparts simply held steady.

These women were often able to break barriers, despite the conservatives in charge at the federal level, because of their allies in the women's movement. Many women who trained in men's professions in the 1970s and 1980s were influenced by the movement; it gave them a sense of entitlement to seats in male-dominated classrooms and the good jobs that followed. Thus, although equal opportunity may have taken a beating at the federal level, it was alive and well in women's consciousness.

But not all women gained equally from education. The earnings gap grew especially rapidly between black and white women at the highest levels of schooling, for reasons which we do not yet fully understand. Clearly, a more permissive environment for racial discrimination exists, due to the decrease in equal opportunity and affirmative action pressure from the federal government in the 1980s. One might also suspect that school quality in segregated schools hurt young black women. But their achievement test scores improved relative to white's, suggesting that if school quality fell, black women simply learned more with less educational resources. Finally, employers do appear to be rewarding high degrees of skill more lucratively nowadays, so that any remaining skill differential between black and white women would generate greater differences in pay.

OUT OF WORK

Changes in the U.S. economy's industrial structure—especially the decline of unionized heavy industry and the rise of wholesale and retail trade—more severely affected the earnings of less educated men than women. Many well-paid jobs previously held by men with a high school degree or less simply disappeared from the industrial landscape. Men who might have found jobs in manufacturing and construction trades 20 years ago now often end up alongside women in the lower-paying wholesale and retail trade industry.

Although deindustrialization has significantly depressed men's earnings, it doesn't seem to be the main reason for the huge wage losses suffered by young non-college educated men. Their displacement from smokestack industries accounts directly for less than half the decline in their real wages. More important was the decline in men's pay within most major industries. Deindustrialization may have contributed to this indirectly, by bringing hundreds of thousands of displaced male workers into competition for the jobs left in other industries. Such "crowding" may have

driven down male wages within trade and services.

While non-college men saw their earnings fall, non-college women had modest increases in their real earnings. The barriers to women in the remaining well-paid blue-collar jobs such as electricians and auto mechanics have barely come down.

Why did the pay gap begin to close suddenly in the 1980s, a decade of unremitting hostility from the federal government?

However, women have benefited from a marked increase in demand for personal services such as hairdressing and laundry and the rise in wholesale and retail trade. For many men, employment in these industries meant downward mobility; for most women, it meant slight advancement.

Consequently, from 1973 to 1986, women in their 20s and 30s with a high school degree saw a 4% raise in their real earnings, to $15,700 for full-time work. That's hardly enough to maintain a family alone, if that need should arise. At the same time, the inflation-adjusted pay of their male counterparts plummeted 16%. A similar, but less pronounced, pattern of change emerged among older workers. Thus, the shrinking pay gap among non-college workers came only in part from these women "catching up" to men; their male counterparts also fell down to them.

WORKING HARDER, GAINING LESS

A striking aspect of the 1980s is the increase in inequality in society as a whole. Whites did better relative to blacks, older workers did better relative to younger, and inequality even increased within education and age groups. As remarkable as the decline in the gender pay gap was, the increase in overall inequality slowed down women's progress toward equality.

To understand this, think of women climbing from near the bottom of a ladder. That ladder stretched longer during the 1980s, putting more distance between the people on the bottom and the people at the top (disproportionately white men). The overall growth in inequality—that is, the greater distance between the top and the bottom rungs—slowed down women's progress. For example, because black women started at the bottom, the overall increase in inequality hurt them more than it hurt white women. It was as if low-paid women workers climbed a rung to higher pay by seeking more education, only to find that they would need to scale many more rungs than before to catch up with workers who had started in the middle or top of the ladder.

Some economists have attributed the greater wage inequality in the United States compared to other highly industrialized countries to the government's extreme "hands off" labor-market policies, which became even more pronounced in the Reagan-Bush years. This insistence on letting markets operate without collective regulation—for example, through affirmative action, unions, comparable worth legislation, social insurance for the poor, or an adequate minimum wage—exacerbates the economic vulnerability of the most marginalized groups in society. With decreased protection for women and people of color, these groups found it much harder to reap the benefits of their own efforts to boost their earnings.

Many women can celebrate big gains in their standard of living, and greater economic independence from men. The young woman who establishes a medical

Ontario's Pay Equity Act

Ontario's Pay Equity Act, passed in 1987, has already proved itself a boon to Canadian women. If, as is likely, amendments significantly extending its coverage are enacted, it will rank as the most effective measure of its kind in the world.

The Act is the first worldwide to require both private- and public-sector employers to pay equal wages to men and women whenever the "compensation-value" of their jobs is equal or comparable. Since its passage, the Act has boosted the wages of thousands of Canadian women. The new amendments would extend coverage to 420,000 additional women at primarily female workplaces such as nursing homes and child-care centers.

The legislation, long advocated by the Equal Pay Coalition (a coalition of Canadian women's and labor groups), aims at rectifying a long-standing injustice: Jobs traditionally held by women often pay less than do those traditionally held by men. For example, secretaries in the United States, 99% of whom are women, earn far less than do mechanics, 97% of whom are men. Although determining a job's compensation-value is difficult and somewhat arbitrary, the Ontario Act sets guidelines designed to make such an evaluation as precise as possible.

Whenever the evaluation system reveals that women earn less than men for jobs of comparable value at the same work site, the employer must raise the women's wages. If female clerical workers in a hospital have been earning a top wage of $8.50 an hour, while male maintenance workers have been earning $9.70 an hour, the hospital is legally bound to close the $1.20 gap if the two jobs are found to be of comparable value. The hospital may **not** cut the men's pay; it may, however, close the pay gap over several years. The act only requires that employers paying inequitable wages reserve 1% of their total payroll each year for pay equity raises.

The law has another important drawback, says Katerina Makovac, an organizer for a Canadian organization advocating pay equity for non-union women. "It is self-managed and complaint-based," she explains. "It is assumed that the employer is following the law unless someone, usually a woman worker, complains. If the workplace is unionized, the union monitors the process. But if no union exists, employers can do almost whatever they want."

How does the evaluation system actually work? Evaluators assign points to each of four main aspects of a job: the degree of skill required, the amount of effort demanded, the share of responsibility borne, and the difficulty of the working conditions involved (for instance, the potential health risks to the worker). They then add the points to determine a job's compensation-value.

If the proposed amendments are enacted, three variants of the evaluation system will be available:

- the basic, job-to-job system (just described), for work sites at which men and women hold comparable jobs;
- the "proportional value" system, for work sites at which men and women hold very different kinds of jobs; and
- the "proxy" system, for public-sector work sites (such as child-care centers and nursing homes) at which only women work.

An evaluator using the proportional-value variant first finds the point total of the male jobs and then determines the ratio of that total to the men's pay. Then the evaluator does the same for women's jobs. If an inequity is found, the employer must henceforth use the men's ratio to determine women's pay.

When no men are employed at a work site, evaluators must use the proxy system: They compare the compensation-value of women's jobs at the site with that of men's jobs at other public-sector work sites.

A recent poll of 1,400 women workers in the United States found that 78% of them were eager to see equal-pay laws enacted in this country. In crafting such legislation, U.S. lawmakers could hardly find a better model than the Ontario Act.

— *Camille Colatosti*

CAMILLE COLATOSTI covers the struggles of women, health-care workers, and workers in other service sectors for *Labor Notes.*

practice is clearly ahead of her mother who could only aspire to a secretary's salary. But other women do not have as much to be happy about. Women without college educations have seen little improvement in their pay, while the earnings of their male kin have been in free fall. Partly because collective institutions are so weak in the United States, and grew even weaker over the 1980s, pay trends were very different for different groups of workers.

Thus, no single answer exists to the question of why women's pay increased relative to men's. So for now, we probably should turn in our 70-cent buttons and hand out many different ones for young women and old women, white women and black women, college-educated women and women with only high school degrees. But most important, we need to remember that the battle for equality isn't over until every women wears a $1.00 button. ∎

Resources: Barbara Bergman, *The Economic Emergence of Women,* 1986; Frank Levy and Richard Michel, *The Economic Future of American Families,* Urban Institute, 1991; Frank Levy and Richard Murnane, "U.S. Earnings Levels and Earnings Inequality: A Review of Recent Trends and Proposed Explanations," *Journal of Economic Literature,* September 1992; Elaine McCrate and Laura Leete-Guy, "Black-White Wage Differences among Young Women, 1977-1986," forthcoming in *Industrial Relations.*

economy in numbers

Dollars & Sense, December 1992

Gender Gaps Galore

Median income of full-time, year-round workers, age 25+, 1989

Male high school grads: $26,600
Female high school grads: $17,500
Male college grads: $38,600
Female college grads: $26,700

Median income of single-parent families, 1989

White male-headed: $30,500
White females: $18,900
Black males: $18,400
Black females: $11,600
Hispanic males: $25,200
Hispanic females: $11,700

Rates of home-ownership for single-parent families, 1990

White males: 53%
White females: 40%
Black males: 39%
Black females: 22%
Hispanic males: 29%
Hispanic females: 21%

Ratio of median housing costs to median income for single-parent families, 1987

Male owners: 17%
Female owners: 19%
Male renters: 31%
Female renters: 43%

Median net worth of single-adult households, 1988

White males: $16,600*
White females: $22,100*
Black males: $1,500
Black females: $800
Hispanic males: $3,000
Hispanic females: $700

Poverty rates of single-parent families with children, 1989

White males: 15%
White females: 36%
Black males: 34%
Black females: 54%
Hispanic males: 27%
Hispanic females: 58%

* Older single white women pull up the median net worth of all single white women. Because a married woman often outlives her spouse, she inherits the couple's accumulated wealth.

Source: Paula Ries & Anne Stone, eds. (for the Women's Research and Education Institute), *The American Woman 1992-93: A Status Report.*

Dollars & Sense, July/August 1991

Earnings Disabilities

Job market undermines education payoff for many

By Randy Albelda

Consider the following: According to the Department of Labor, demand for sales clerks, waiters and waitresses, clerical help, janitors, cashiers, and food-counter workers places these six low-skill jobs among the fastest growing occupations in the U.S..

If you were talking to a young person entering high school now, what advice would you give about the value of education? Finish high school and then get an available job in one of these rapidly expanding service fields? Perhaps. But your advice would be less sage than it would have been 10 years earlier, particularly if your friend is an African-American male.

Unfortunately, for all the exhortations not to drop out of school, a high school diploma won't get him nearly what it would have in the late 1970s. The high-wage union jobs in manufacturing that used to give male high school graduates a decent life have been replaced by low-paying jobs in the service sector.

What's more, discrimination, both in the job market and in higher education, continues to play a strong role in determining who gets what job, often overriding the qualifications attained through education. Despite women's wage advances relative to men's, the average college-educated woman still earns less than the average high school-educated man.

RANDY ALBELDA, a member of the *Dollars & Sense* Collective, teaches economics at the University of Massachusetts-Boston.

Education has always been considered a one-way ticket up the socioeconomic ladder, and educational opportunities have indeed expanded. During the past two decades, a larger percentage of Americans have attended and completed college than at any time in the past. Women, people of color, and working-class families fought long, hard battles in the 1950s, 1960s, and 1970s to promote both financial and physical access to education in order to improve their economic opportunities. Desegregation, the expansion of state university systems, federal scholarship programs, and coeducation changed the make-up of schoolyards and college campuses.

A TERRIBLE THING TO WASTE

A mind may be "a terrible thing to waste," but what does the job market offer those young people of color and children of working class families who are once again struggling with questions of access in this age of soaring tuitions, shrinking financial aid pools, and spreading budgetary restraint? The clarity of the answers depends on race and gender. For while education helps a person get ahead, it doesn't help as much as it used to. And the expansion of educational opportunity clearly hasn't eliminated inequality.

A close look at the earnings of workers by race, age, and gender indicates that white men—regardless of age and schooling—still get more for their education buck than do men of color or women. Graph 1 depicts the average earnings of year-round, full-time workers in six demographic groups at three different levels of educational attainment—less than 12

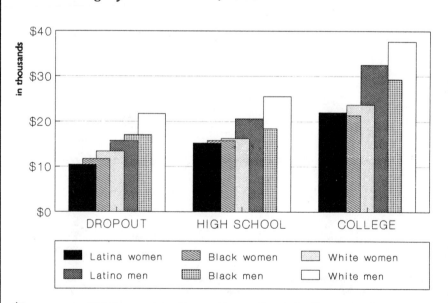

Graph 1: The education pay-off
Mean earnings by education level, 1987*

in thousands

Legend:
- Latina women
- Latino men
- Black women
- Black men
- White women
- White men

*For year-round full-time workers. Source: Current Population Survey data, by author.

years (a high school dropout), 12 years of school, and four years of college.

As the graph shows, college graduates have relatively brighter futures than people with less education, but education better illuminates some futures than others. A "white-male premium" exists at every educational level. For example, the average white male college graduate earned $6,000 more in 1987 than the average comparably educated Latino man, $8,000 more than his black male counterpart, and $13,000 more than a comparable white woman.

These results fly in the face of one of today's prevailing economic theories, which claims productivity—based on a worker's investment in education and self-improvement, not skin color or gender—determines wages. This so-called human-capital theory attributes racial and sexual wage differences to a lack of personal investment and commitment (see box).

LOUSY PAY FOR LOUSY JOBS

According to the "human capitalists," the wage gap should have dissolved as people of color and women invested more in a college education. It hasn't. In fact, the dollar gap between white men and most other groups is widest for those with a college degree. Why doesn't education pay off evenly? Because—contrary to the assertions of the human-capital school—the characteristics of jobs, not simply the skills of people that fill them, help determine wages. Since white men still have better access to good jobs, self-acquired endowments like education and experience don't pay off equally. For education to deliver an equitable payoff, well-paid jobs would have to be allocated equally.

Employers and male workers have long benefited from the inequitable distribution of jobs and from women's low wages. Companies, benefiting from lower wages, and predominantly male unions, protecting their members from job competition, helped route women into only a few occupations, like secretary, teacher, nurse, sales person, and service worker. These jobs and industries pay considerably less than manufacturing, construction, transportation, and other male-dominated industries—regardless of the skills required.

Exclusionary practices have also kept

men of color out of many well-paying jobs. African-American and Latino men have a harder time landing the better jobs, are often assigned to the lower rungs of job ladders, and receive little chance for upward mobility. Women of color, who have gained some ground relative to white women, are still slotted into the worst paying of all jobs.

Despite legal restrictions, there's ample evidence that many employers still discriminate. A recent study by the Washington-based Urban Institute demonstrated the difficulty educated black men face on the job market: One out of five times, white men advanced further in the application process than similarly qualified black men.

For working people, gains in earnings hardly reflected the significant educational advances they made in the 1980s. In 1987, close to 81% of all persons between the ages 18 and 65 had completed high school, up from 75% in 1979. Those with some college education jumped from 35% in 1979 to 40% in 1987. Yet earnings of this better-educated work force barely kept pace with inflation. The average earnings of year-round, full-time workers in 1987 was less than half a percent higher than the average in 1979.

The earnings story is, however, more nuanced than those numbers alone suggest. During the 1980s, the stock of de-

Improving "human capital"

A mind isn't a terrible thing to waste, according to human-capital theorists. Under the right circumstances, wasting it might be a perfectly rational choice.

Human-capital theory argues that individual investments in education or on-the-job training directly improve one's productivity. The more productive a worker, the higher the worker's earnings.

University of Chicago economist Gary Becker introduced human-capital theory in the 1970s as a way to explain wage differences among workers, superseding the discrimination models he pioneered in the 1960s.

A linchpin of the human-capital school is that people rationally choose between staying in school and entering the job market. Any individual, after considering the costs of school and the foregone income, will decide whether it is "worth" going to school. That is, will a lifetime's earnings with more schooling, minus the direct and indirect costs of getting that education, surpass lifetime earnings with less education?

According to human capitalists, the answer to this question is more likely "no" for women and people of color than it is for white men. Women's education doesn't pay off,

they argue, because they leave work to have and raise children. This biological "fact" results in less personal investment since the skills won't be used and there is an actual erosion of skills when women leave the paid labor force, as well as a loss of valuable experience. Together, these reduce productivity and with it wages. Men of color, they argue, choose not to pursue more education because they place a premium on earnings today rather than in the future.

In this way, human-capital theory places the cause of wage differentials squarely on the individual's shoulders rather than on access, cost, and discrimination both in the education system and the job market. Human-capital theorists reject any discussion of institutional barriers that different groups face—providing intellectual ammunition to conservative policy-makers.

However, a large number of economic studies have shown that only a small portion of the wage gap between men and women and between whites and people of color can be explained by differences in education and experience. Discrimination by employers, other workers, and educators are more likely explanations for wage differentials.

Graph 2: Change in earnings, 1979-1987

Change in average real earnings for workers aged 25-44*

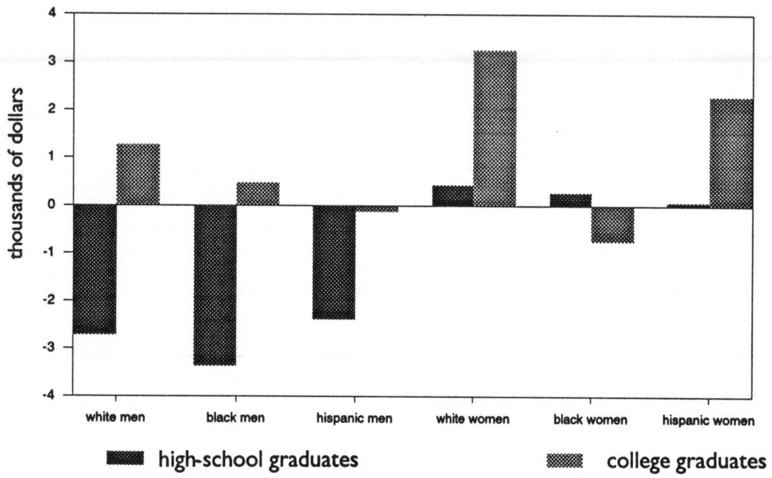

* For year-round, full-time workers.
Source: Current Population Survey data, by author.

cent jobs for high school-educated workers shrank. But since most of these jobs were in male-dominated manufacturing industries, men were the ones to lose ground, men of color fastest of all. Partly as a result of men's decline, women now earn 65% instead of 59% of the average male wage.

Graph 2 compares inflation-adjusted earnings in 1987 with those in 1979 for high school-educated year-round, full-time workers between the ages of 25 and 44. It does the same for workers with college degrees. These workers have generally completed their education, are in their prime earning years, and are more likely than older workers to have benefited from the gains of the civil rights and feminist movements.

During that period, men saw their average real earnings erode. Black and Latino men lost more than white men. Meanwhile women, led by white women, experienced rising earnings. Men's losses are largely attributable to setbacks suffered by those without college degrees. Improved earnings for women with college degrees lifted women as a group. Changes in the economy and the job market—the rather rapid evaporation of unionized manufacturing jobs, the growth of white-collar middle-management service jobs, and the unionization of traditional women's professional jobs—help explain these wage trends.

Many well-paying blue-collar jobs, requiring no more than a high school education, vanished during the 1980s: Man-

ufacturing employment fell by close to 10% during the period in question, accounting for the earnings losses for high school-educated men. Since high-paying manufacturing jobs offered women limited opportunity, the decline of manufacturing hasn't hit the earnings of similarly educated women nearly as hard as it hit those of men.

Access to college also produced uneven results. College-educated white and Latina women earned substantially more, and white and black men gained a bit. But college-educated Latino men and black women suffered relative losses *vis-á-vis* their high school-educated compatriots.

Trends in labor organizing help explain women's collective advance. Unionization in traditionally female jobs increased during the 1980s and is paying off in the form of higher wages. Unions representing teachers, clerical, and health workers—frequently college-educated women—have attracted many new members since 1979, bucking an economy-wide trend against unions.

The growth of the service sector further explains college-educated women's gains and male high-school graduates' losses. The service industry tends to create two types of jobs: low-paying, low-skill jobs like flipping hamburgers and taking tickets in movie theaters, and higher-paying management jobs in legal, financial, and health services, jobs that usually require a college degree.

High school-educated men—notably former manufacturing workers and their

sons—are increasingly taking the first type of job. The low-level service jobs provide women with just more of the same, but for men they're a step down. Similarly, for women with college degrees, the second type of jobs represent real employment gains both in access and wages. For men with college degrees, middle-management jobs in the service sector are—at best—no better than the jobs they would have held in the past.

TICKET TO RIDE?

Falling incomes and employer worries about the decline in the number of qualified workers has generated a debate about reforming primary and secondary education. This debate should be broadened to include the quality of jobs available and access to higher education.

Young people are facing some very tough economic circumstances that will affect and be affected by the decisions they make about their education. Is it worth it to finish high school? When should they enter the labor market? How can they go to college?

There is no doubt that increasingly both men and women need a college degree to earn a decent living and, if they choose, support a family. But the cost of a college education has soared. One year's tuition with room and board at Harvard, Yale, and other private universities now exceeds $20,000. Public universities charge close to $8,000 for a year's tuition, fees, room, and board.

Access to higher education should be a right rather than a privilege. Higher education allows workers of all races and genders to improve their status. But that alone won't solve the problems of wage inequality and overall decline. Only changes in the wage structure and expanded access to all jobs will do this.

Furthermore, the problem is not that being sales clerks and food preparers and servers lacks skill or even dignity. The real issue lies with the fact that these jobs pay poorly and deliver few benefits—like health insurance and pensions. Rather than doom a generation to lousy paying jobs, workers must force service-sector employers to pay more. Not unlike manufacturing jobs in the 1920s, employers will not be induced to increase productivity in these sectors until they are required to pay workers better. ∎

Dollars & Sense, September 1988

What Future for Unions?

Labor leaders offer a different view of the labor market

By Patricia Horn

As the Reagan era draws to a close, the labor movement is heaving a sigh of relief. In the last eight years, unions have suffered at the hands of a strongly anti-union president who baptized his administration with the dramatic firing of the striking air-traffic controllers. Unions have watched the Reagan administration reshape the National Labor Relations Board (NLRB) with anti-labor appointments which dramatically weakened the effectiveness of the National Labor Relations Act (NLRA).

But the Reagan administration is not the only cause of a diminished labor movement. A new administration will not solve many of labor's problems. Since several years before Reagan took office, management has increasingly shown success at opposing unionization and stymying traditional organizing tactics. The percentage of unionized workers has dropped dramatically since the mid-1970s. Even before the 1970s, that percentage fell gradually but consistently from its peak of nearly 40% in the early 1950s. Internally, unions have debated a host of issues, including whether to engage in concession bargaining, how closely to collaborate with employers in the workplace, and how to bring more women and people of color into union leadership.

The pulse of the labor movement is its organizers. They are the union representatives who experience on a daily basis the success or failure of their organizing campaigns. To get

*a sense of labor's future, **Dollars & Sense** posed a series of questions to five organizers. They discuss the impact that stronger federal government and management opposition has had on organizing, highlighting the creative responses organizers are now employing. They address other causes of labor's continued decline, including the need for a stronger political voice and the effect of changes in the work force. And they assess the future of unions. While many labor watchers have pronounced unions a dying breed, these organizers see signs of new life in the labor movement. Below we print excerpts from their responses.* ■

VIRGINIA DIAMOND
AFL-CIO

Virginia Diamond, a former organizer with the International Ladies Garment Workers Union (ILGWU), is now the national organizing coordinator for the AFL-CIO's Organizing Department. The Organizing Department publishes two newsletters for organizers. The "Report on Union Busters" chronicles the activities of anti-union consultants, and the "Statistical and Tactical Information Report" details successful organizing tactics.

Beginning in the mid-1970s, anti-union campaigns and the anti-union consultant industries mushroomed. In the past, campaigns were much less intensive, less sophisticated, and the use of consultants less pervasive. Now, every time an election petition is filed, employers get dozens of letters from these consultants soliciting business. They whip the employers into a frenzy over the dire consequences of employees forming a union.

These consultants have studied the NLRA, tested its limits, and uncovered all of the weaknesses inherent in the law that employers may not have been as aware of. Consultants make a lot of money off this. It's not unknown for a company to spend $100,000 fighting a union.

One of the features of a consultant's campaign is training supervisors to conduct intensive, one-on-one, high-pressure conversations with all of the employees in their unit. Production can come almost to a halt and the entire operation is geared to campaigning against the union eight hours a day, five days a week. Supervisors are coached to look for the employee's weak spot and to prey upon it.

Employers play heavily upon the false notion that unions are constantly going on strike, even though less than 1% of contract negotiations end up in strikes. They will come up with volumes of pages filled with pictures and articles and stories about strikes and imply to people that if they form a union the company won't bargain and they will have no other choice but to strike. They use leaflets, letters, posters, speeches, and movies. The people really forget why they wanted to form a union in the first place and think, "Thank God I have a job." It's psychological warfare. You really need to live through it to understand why many of us feel that it's remarkable that we ever win at organizing elections.

While the percentage of unionized workers was in decline, we tended to concentrate on ways to protect our current membership. Organizing, because it is so costly and so difficult, wasn't as much of a priority. Now we have learned that in order to protect the standard of living and working conditions of our members, we must constantly reach out to non-members. Besides, it is part of our mandate and mission to reach out to all working people. At times, the labor movement was naive. There was a sense that companies were willing to accept our existence. We've learned the hard way that many employers were scheming behind the scenes to obliterate the gains we were making. But we think we've bottomed out. We're optimistic about the future.

PATRICIA HORN is a *Dollars & Sense* editor.

JAMES ORANGE
Industrial Union Dept., AFL-CIO

James Orange began working in the civil rights movement two decades ago. He has organized for the Southern Christian Leadership Conference (SCLC) and for the Amalgamated Clothing and Textile Workers Union. He now organizes new locals for the Industrial Union Department of the AFL-CIO in Georgia.

The NLRB and the NLRA are the most important things we have to change that are against workers today. The whole NLRA has been relaxed. Five years ago, it was illegal for a supervisor to walk up to a worker and start discussing with him why he was for the union or why he had on a union t-shirt. Today it is just another conversation. Workers are being terminated more frequently for their union involvement. Today we are not winning as many of those cases as we won 10-15 years ago.

Management uses the community very well and they have been using the community for years. You go to a lot of rural communities and management sponsors the church programs. Management will go to the newspaper and the newspaper writes anti-union articles. Management deals with a lot of community businesses. The bank will foreclose on loans or not give people credit who are up front for the union. Management has workers do surveillance on other workers and report to them who the union supporters are. Before the Reagan administration, you didn't have as much going on because management knew that the labor board would find them guilty. Now you are not getting as much support out of the board.

But there is no question unions are coming back. Normally you go out and look for the campaign. But when you get 10, 15, or 20 calls a day from workers who have never organized before saying they want an organizer, that tells you that interest in unions is increasing instead of declining. Workers know they cannot get any respect on the job, any dignity on the job, better wages, better working conditions, any health insurance, unless they organize. The Reagan crunch has touched folks down here. Workers are feeling now that the only protection they can have is through organizing and having the union.

Unions have to take a political role, they have to take a role in the community, they have to take a role on social issues, they have to be in coalitions. Because the same enemies I have in the labor movement, Joe Lowery at the SCLC has in the civil rights movement; and the same enemies I have in the labor movement, the ladies now have in the women's movement; the same enemies I have in the labor movement, the environmentalists now have in their movement. We have to start forming coalitions and working better and closer together with our allies.

York, Chicago, San Francisco. But as buildings went up in suburbs and the South we rarely organized them, so as a percentage of the industry we declined. That weakened us dramatically. As the problems mounted, we didn't do enough to combat the growing power of management.

In the late 1970s, there were downturns in the real estate industry—vacancy rates rose—so management had more incentive to come after us. We were much weaker because we had not kept up with changes in the work force. The work force was now overwhelmingly minority

> ## Unions have to take a political role, a role in the community, a role on social issues, and they have to build coalitions.
> ### — James Orange

STEPHEN LERNER
Justice for Janitors

Stephen Lerner is currently the director of Building Services Organizing of the Service Employees International Union (SEIU). He organizes their Justice for Janitors campaign.

I think we deceive ourselves when we act like the only reason labor is in trouble is because of Reagan coming to power or changes in the NLRB or the growing management opposition. I think Reagan and union busters exacerbate the problem, but if you really look at the post-World War II era, we've been totally unsuccessful at keeping up with the growth in our industries. Though our membership may have slowly increased, we've been on a decline as a percentage of the work force since the fifties. The setbacks of labor during the 1970s and 1980s are more a result of a gradual weakening in labor. We haven't successfully organized for 30 years and we're paying the price for that.

In the case of low-wage service workers and in the case of janitors, we had a traditional base in certain cities—New

and, in some areas, overwhelmingly Hispanic. There's no doubt management came after us incredibly hard and successfully took whole cities non-union and exacted huge concessions from us.

We made the official turnaround in our union in 1986. The union instituted a national rebuilding program that called for a nationwide campaign to fight for justice for janitors. We've been massively successful. We look at Justice for Janitors not as traditional organizing but as movement building. Janitors are the newest immigrants, they are minorities, they are overwhelmingly poor and overwhelmingly women.

Our basic strategy is going after whole geographic areas simultaneously instead of just one building. The only way to affect wage rates is to control a whole city and have a standard wage rate that everyone bids. A key part of union strength has always come from controlling the majority of an industry. That was a CIO strategy in basic industries like autos and steel, and that is our strategy with janitors.

Whenever possible, we stay away from NLRB elections. We go directly to the building owners and the contractors employed by the building owner and we say, "A majority of your workers want the union." Then, in a variety of ways, we try to pressure them into recognizing us without going to the NLRB. We use lots and lots of civil disobedience. We do sit-ins in buildings, pray-ins, elevator-jams. We do 24 hour vigils—a lot of things in the tradition of civil rights and the farm workers union. We run very, very, visible and vocal up-front campaigns. I think one of the key problems in the labor movement and every movement is that everyone is searching for the one tactic that works. I don't think there is any one tactic that works. What we need to find is many tactics that work in combination.

I don't think we can talk about the future of unions as a whole. The turn-around depends on the industry. Throughout the labor movement there are many unions and organizers that are getting results. In specific industries and specific unions and specific regions we are finding the right way to do things. It's encouraging that we are organizing workers, having militant struggles, and winning decent contracts creatively.

KATIE QUAN
ILGWU

Katie Quan is the Assistant Director of the New York Metro Organizing Department of the ILGWU. In 1981, she organized a group of rank-and-file garment workers to lobby for the creation of a day-care center in Chinatown jointly funded by employers and New York City.

The ILGWU has had to keep up with the changing work force. We started out as a union of mostly Italian and Jewish immigrants. In the 1940s and 1950s, there were a lot of black workers. In the 1950s and 1960s, the main flow was from Puerto Rico. Now in the 1980s, the workers have come from Central and South America and Asia. We've had to hire organizers who reflect who the workers are. In my department every person speaks two languages, some speak three. We have Chinese, Korean, Puerto Rican, Dominican, and Honduran organizers.

Some unions tend to only take care of shop situations and not realize that for someone who has a kid and no one to take care of her, that's a crisis. A lot of unions will say that's none of our busi-

ness. But any good organizer has to make a difference in what people feel is vital and critical to their own lives—whether that is in the shop or with the family or community.

A lot of us are beginning to realize that the bread and butter issues are not the only way to organize workers. My effort in organizing the day-care center shows that issues that relate to family and community are important. Certainly, the women who were in the organizing committee for the day-care center weren't initially the most active trade unionists. After the day-care center was set up, they became active trade unionists.

The same goes with community and labor organizing. Most of our members are immigrants from other countries who relate strongly to ethnic communities. The ILGWU has a heavy presence in Chinatown. Of the 450 shops in Chinatown, 99% of them are union shops. The union participates heavily in anti-gentrification organizing, election of local representatives, in movements against a jail being built in the heart of Chinatown, and for space for non-profit buildings. Whenever there's a coalition in Chinatown, the union is always asked to participate.

Unions should really become more a part of the life of the workers in the rank and file, and the rank and file should take a more active role in union affairs. That would be true union democracy.

STEVE EARLY
CWA

Steve Early has been active in the labor movement since 1972. He is currently an International Representative for the Communications Workers of America and has worked on the national staff of the United Mine Workers. He is also a lawyer and labor journalist.

The biggest single obstacle we face is workers' understandable fear of being fired and the knowledge more and more workers have that, at this point, the NLRA protections against discrimination for union activity are very minimal. The whole direction of labor law has been increasingly hostile to unionization. The NLRB is just about useless—and worse than useless when it becomes a tool of the employers in representation elections and unfair labor practice proceedings.

Unorganized workers are aware of the lost strike trend, the seeming inability of unions to resist concession demands, or to win strikes in bargaining units where they've had an established bargaining re-

Labor in the eighties

One of the challenges facing the labor movement in the 1990s is to redress the setbacks of the '80s. Employers not only flattened but actually reduced real wages, slashed benefits, and passed on more costs to workers. The numbers tell the story:

• Real hourly earnings in private, non-farm employment fell 6.4% from 1979 to 1989.

• In contracts negotiated in 1983, 37% of private, non-farm workers and 56% of manufacturing workers took freezes or cuts. For manufacturing workers the worst year was 1986 when 60% took freezes or cuts. Even in 1989, the seventh year of the economic

"recovery," 10% of all workers and 17% of manufacturing workers with new contracts took freezes or cuts.

• Among workers covered by major labor contracts, the percentage that had cost-of-living adjustment clauses fell from 59% in 1979 to 40% in 1989.

• The percentage of workers with fully paid health plans fell from 72% in 1980 to 45% in 1986.

• From 1986 to 1989, payroll deductions for health plans have increased 12% for individual coverage and 19% for family coverage. Deductibles for family plans rose an average of 6.5% in the same period.

lationship for years. It's a hard job to convince any group of people that you can build an organization from scratch in a non-union workplace—particularly a big hospital or high tech corporation—that would ever become strong enough to overcome management's intense hostility to workers' self-organization. People today don't have a sense that, as recently as 50 years ago, workers were able to build entire industrial unions from the bottom up through their own mass activity.

During the last 10 to 20 years, unionism has been rising or holding fairly steady in Canada at 35-40% of the work force. It's half that here. One difference is that 25 years ago the Canadian Labor Congress took the initiative to build a labor-oriented third party—the New Democratic Party. Because most labor relations issues and other social welfare programs are province-level matters, unions have been able to enact very favorable legislation on workers' rights, pay equity, plant closing, and even employers' use of scabs in some provinces. Unlike here, Canadians have also done better in organizing the service and retail sectors and other expanding segments of the economy. A lot of people point to the better labor laws as the difference between the U.S. and Canada, but that begs the question of where labor laws come from. In Canada, they're a product of independent labor politics pursued through the New Democratic Party.

Labor here ought to be getting behind legislation that would provide due process for all workers. That would demonstrate that unions are on the side of workers whether they are dues-payers or not, and that organized labor is the only force in society that can provide an effective counterweight to the growing power of management. I don't think anyone can assume that simply putting Dukakis in the White House will automatically change the current climate. If you look at history, it took major upheavals to force Franklin Roosevelt to aid labor's cause in the 1930s. It's going to take similar rank-and-file pressure and disruption of "industrial peace" before unions begin to regain the ground they've lost since the protections of the New Deal have crumbled under the employer assaults and rollbacks of Reaganism. ■

Dollars & Sense, December 1989

No Voice for Workers

U.S. economy penalizes worker participation

By David I. Levine & Laura D'Andrea Tyson

Japan does it. Sweden does it. Some U.S. corporations even do it. It's not revolutionary, it may not even be radical, but chances are it will increase productivity where implemented. "It" is increased worker participation—giving workers a substantive say in the production process, including training new employees, dealing directly with suppliers, setting the work pace, and keeping the firm's financial records.

Most studies show increased worker participation leads to greater productivity or output per hour of labor (see box). But if worker participation increases productivity, why is it so rare in the United States? Mainstream economists—a skeptical bunch—conclude that the scarcity of participatory arrangements in this country proves their inefficiency. If participation were such a good idea, they argue, then firms that didn't allow participation would tend to perform worse than firms that did. Eventually, the non-participatory firms would go out of business.

In fact, overall economic conditions in the United States, as well as the current

DAVID I. LEVINE teaches industrial relations at the University of California, Berkeley, and is a *Dollars & Sense* editorial associate. LAURA D'ANDREA TYSON teaches economics at the University of California, Berkeley. A longer version of this article appears in *Paying for Productivity*, edited by Alan S. Blinder (Brookings Institution, 1989).

rarity of worker participation, combine to form an environment hostile to worker participation. What mainstream economists leave out is that the success of worker participation depends not just on the actions of an isolated firm, but also on overall economic conditions and other firms' actions. From the point of view of the individual company, worker participation is easiest to implement when the national unemployment rate is stable and low, when other firms also allow worker participation, and when financial markets are oriented toward long-term investment. It is therefore possible that workers, capitalists, and consumers would all be better off in an economy with lots of worker participation, yet each individual firm would find it unprofitable to allow participation on its own.

A PARTICIPATORY PARABLE

To illustrate the point, imagine two fictitious auto plants with very different work organizations. The first plant, Swedish Auto (SA) uses a highly participatory work organization. It has the three characteristics necessary to guarantee worker support for participation: profit-sharing, long-term job security, and a narrow range of wages between the highest and lowest paid workers. Its competitor, Farmingham, uses a traditional labor system and has none of these characteristics.

Both plants set wages once a year. Farmingham lays off workers whenever the economy slows down and the demand for new cars drops off. SA, on the other hand, has pledged not to lay off workers. During downturns, SA stops hiring new workers, trains current workers who have spare time due to a reduced work load, and transfers workers from production jobs to maintenance tasks.

When recessions are frequent and deep, Farmingham's use of layoffs saves the company money. The company doesn't have to worry about paying workers during slow periods, as does SA. On the other hand, SA's no-layoff pledge and long-term employment relations are more beneficial when recessions are shallow or infrequent. As a consequence, SA-type firms will flourish in economies characterized by stable growth and only minor fluctuations in demand.

Each firm's employment system, in turn, affects the economy as a whole. When many firms use layoffs during economic downturns, recessions tend to be deeper. Farmingham's now unemployed workers buy fewer consumer goods. The result is further layoffs at stores in the Farmingham area. Eventually consumer-goods manufacturers elsewhere feel the impact as well. When most firms avoid layoffs, however, recessions tend to be shallower and shorter-lived. Since the costs of worker participation increase

with the instability of the economy, macroeconomic policies that moderate the ups and downs of the economy create a favorable environment for participatory work arrangements.

The level of economy-wide unemployment affects the success of individual firms' worker participation efforts, and is in turn affected by them. Farmingham uses fear of dismissal to discipline its workers. This is relatively inexpensive when unemployment is high because workers know they cannot easily find another job. When unemployment drops, however, absenteeism and turnover at Farmingham rise, and productivity and quality decline. SA uses participation, profit-sharing, and workers' monitoring each other to motivate workers. Correspondingly, productivity at SA stays high even when unemployment is low.

If most firms use a Farmingham-type system, the economy will tend to generate a high level of unemployment. The reason is that low unemployment is incompatible with a labor system that relies on fear of dismissal to keep workers on their toes. In such economies, a drop in unemployment will eventually lead to an increase in wages. This raises costs and causes profits to fall. When profits fall,

capitalists generally invest less, building fewer new plants and buying less equipment. That in turn leads to lower demand for labor and an increase in unemployment. So in this sense, the system creates what it needs to survive: when high unemployment is necessary to motivate workers, unemployment will tend to stay high. The U.S. economy is a prime example of this phenomenon.

In contrast, low unemployment and tight labor markets are sustainable if all firms use participation. Since worker motivation does not depend on the threat of dismissal, tight labor markets will not inevitably lead to declines in profits and investment (and increases in wages and turnover). In fact, participation may be necessary for unemployment to stay low over the long term.

As this parable demonstrates, the type of work organization new firms choose will depend partly on the tightness of the existing labor market. When average unemployment rates are low for a long time, participatory work organizations become more attractive as ways to motivate and retain workers.

In Sweden, for example, the government has consistently held the unemployment rate below 3%. According to one Swedish expert, this has "increased rates of turnover and absenteeism in monotonous, exhausting, and dirty jobs to the point that job redesign and increasing worker satisfaction become vital for any manager who wants to maintain a stable, competent labor force." That is, at low levels of unemployment, firms find it necessary to make work motivating to maintain productivity.

REDUCING WAGE DIFFERENTIALS

The spread between high and low wages within a firm similarly affects the viability of worker participation. In a traditional work place, wide wage differentials are an important motivating factor. In contrast, participatory firms reduce status and wage differentials to increase worker unity. Such firms eliminate reserved parking places, executive dining rooms, and other status-building perks.

Reducing the spread between wages has two consequences for SA. First, overall worker productivity generally rises as worker participation and motivation increase. Since the lowest-paid workers re-

Participation and productivity

The authors recently surveyed the existing research on worker participation. They found that involving workers in the production process usually produces small short-run improvements in productivity, sometimes leads to significant, long-lasting improvements, and almost never leads to reductions in productivity. The survey covers over 40 empirical studies from diverse journals and publications in a variety of fields, including econometrics, psychology, and industrial management.

The form and content of worker participation has a significant impact on its likelihood of raising productivity. In particular, worker participation increases pro-

ductivity most when it involves substantive participation in shop floor decisions rather than consultative arrangements such as quality circles. Token worker ownership (as in employee stock ownership plans) and representative participation (having a single worker on the company's board of directors, for example) raises productivity by very little, and not for sustained periods of time. The substantive participation that has a more lasting impact on productivity includes formal, direct arrangements, such as work teams. Typically, workers in work teams make their own work assignments and determine their own work routines.

73

Carol ✷ Simpson © 1988

ceive wages higher than the going rate, SA will attract good workers at the low end of the wage scale, who will stay with the company for longer stretches. On the other hand, the highest-paid workers—from skilled workers up through top management—receive wages lower than the going market rate. This policy will be most costly to SA when other firms offer a wide wage dispersion. Those firms will tend to attract SA's "stars"—its most skilled workers.

If Farmingham and other firms also have narrow wage and status differentials, however, SA can keep its stars. In that case, all firms benefit from the increased participation and productivity.

CAPITAL MARKETS

The success of worker participation also depends on conditions in capital markets—where firms arrange to borrow the funds they need to do business. SA faces two main problems when it goes looking for investment funds. Banks, stockholders, and other investment brokers prefer

to invest in tangible assets. They fear that when managers claim to be investing in intangibles (such as a long-term cozy relationship with workers) they might in fact be covering up their own incompetence or simply investing in assets with a low payoff. Since the participatory style of firms like SA requires investments in areas that are difficult to monitor (like worker skills and worker commitment), these capital markets tend to be biased against them.

Hostile takeovers and leveraged buyouts also undermine SA's ability to build a long-term reputation of trustworthiness with its workers. Many takeovers lead to huge layoffs and drastic changes in work-place organization. When a takeover's immediate profits come from reneging on promises to workers, other firms have a harder time succeeding with strategies based on high commitment to their workers.

Capital markets in the United States generally encourage investors to seek short-term gains rather than longstand-

ing relations with individual firms. These markets are better suited to serve traditional work places than participatory ones.

Our arguments suggest that under certain conditions, the market system may be systematically biased against participatory work places. Despite the potential economy-wide productivity gains made possible by such work places, product, labor, and capital markets can all make participation unprofitable for the individual firm. As a result, the entire economy can be trapped in an undesirable position.

Economists, corporate managers, and the business press have looked just about everywhere for a solution to the "productivity puzzle," but the answer may lie in their own back yard. Until policy-makers alter the external conditions facing firms—high unemployment, economic instability, and capital markets oriented to the very short term—worker participation will remain rare in the United States, and so will the productivity gains associated with it. ∎

When Markets Don't Work

Dollars & Sense, March 1990

What's Work Got To Do With It?

Work alone won't lift poor families out of poverty

By Randy Albelda & Chris Tilly

Conservatives offer a simple explanation for why some families end up in poverty while others don't: Poor men and women don't work hard enough, and poor women don't manage to get married and stay married. "The requirements for getting out of poverty in this country are...minimal," maintains neoconservative sociologist Charles Murray, and the top requirement is to "get a job, any job, and stick with the labor market."

"That's ridiculous!" says Diane Dujon of the National Welfare Rights Union, a ten-year veteran of the welfare rights movement and a former welfare recipi-

RANDY ALBELDA, a member of the *Dollars & Sense* Collective, teaches economics at the University of Massachusetts at Boston. CHRIS TILLY, also a member of the *Dollars & Sense* Collective, teaches economics at the University of Lowell in Massachusetts.

ent herself. "There are structural reasons why people are poor: They have the worst education and the lowest-paying jobs. Single mothers end up poor because women just don't earn what men earn on the job market. Plus they have the additional problem of taking care of children."

Our research shows she's right. We recently completed a study in which we looked at why certain types of families are especially likely to be poor. For example, why did 43% of families headed by single mothers fall below the poverty line in 1987, compared to only 5% of families with two adults and no children? We found that hard work is not a route to prosperity for most poor families, because these families lack sufficient workers to place in the labor market, and because those who do find jobs find only low-wage jobs.

Conservatives have called for welfare "reform"—including reduced benefit levels, tightened eligibility rules, and stricter work requirements—and Congress has enacted many of these proposals over the last ten years, most recently in the Family Support Act of 1988. But our research suggests that since the majority of the poor are not in a position to work their way out of poverty, such policy changes simply leave poor families worse off.

Particularly critical to a family's income level are family members' gender and age, the total number of working-age adults, and the number of children. To find out just how family make-up affects income, we grouped U.S. families into seven types (see box). Using data for 1973, 1979, and 1987, we adjusted family income to correct for family size and inflation. The income adjustment means that we measure income in "need" units rather than dollars—with one unit equal to the poverty line for a given family type. Unless otherwise stated, all income comparisons in this article are made on the basis of these need units rather than raw income.

As might be expected, the income differences between family types are stark. *DINC* households (double income, no children) pocketed more than three times as much adjusted income as single mothers—*Moms*. How much of the gap is due to effort, and how much to disparate numbers of working-age adults and wage levels? The answer comes from a closer look at families' sources of income.

BRINGING HOME THE BACON

Family income includes both earnings (wages and self-employment income) and unearned income (property income, alimony and child support, and government assistance). Differences in earnings provide the key to income disparities among the seven family types, since earn-

Family types and income sources

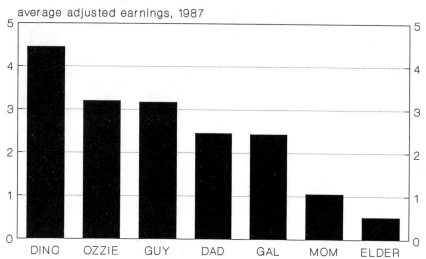

average adjusted earnings, 1987

In this article, we examine family income by type of family and by source of income using Census Bureau data from the Current Population Survey. To allow meaningful comparisons between families and over time, we adjusted income to take into account family size and inflation. We looked at 1973, 1979 and 1987 because these three years correspond roughly to the last year of the economic boom over the last three business cycles in the United States, making them the most appropriate years to compare during the 1970s and 1980s.

Income sources We distinguished four sources of income: earnings from work or self employment; income from property, savings, and pensions; child support and alimony; and government-provided income. The above graph shows adjusted earnings by family type for 1987.

Family types We divided the families into seven types, distinguished by the number of adults, the presence of children under 18, and the age and gender of the head of the household. The percentage of families in each type in 1987 are in parentheses.

DINC—two or more adults, no children, head under 65 (short for "Double Income, No Children") (21%)

Ozzie—two or more adults of any age, with at least one child (named in honor of Ozzie and Harriet) (28%)

Guy—one male adult under 65, no children (13%)

Gal—one female adult under 65, no children (11%)

Mom—one female adult, any age, with at least one child (6%)

Dad—one male adult, any age, with at least one child (1%)

Elder—head of family 65 or older, no children (20%)

Income adjustment In order to adjust for inflation and take into account different income needs based on family size, we divided each family's income by its poverty line. The Census Bureau calculates the poverty line for a family based on the number of adults, children, and persons over 65, and adjusts the line annually by the average inflation rate. For example, in 1987 the average poverty line was $8,282 for *DINCs*, $11,871 for *Ozzies*, and $9,164 for *Moms*. A family with an adjusted income of 2.0 has a dollar income equal to twice its poverty line.

ings account for 77% of the average family's income.

Earnings differences among family types have been large and stable during the 1970s and 1980s. In fact, the ranking of family types from highest- to lowest-earning did not budge between 1973 and 1987.

Earnings are largest for families with working-age male adults (see graph). This includes husband-wife families (*DINCs* and *Ozzies*) as well as families headed by a single man (*Guys* and *Dads*).

The presence of children reduces adjusted earnings. Two-parent families with children earn only 70% of what those without children earn. Among female-headed households, *Moms* (single mothers) earn much less than *Gals* (single women with no children).

Finally, families headed by people over 65 have the lowest earnings, although not the lowest incomes. Of all the family types, their incomes are supplemented most by unearned income, mainly government transfers.

Most of the differences in earnings between family types result from the different amount of labor families supply. When we broke down those differences, we found that family types who work less do so because they have fewer available workers—not because of laziness or welfare dependence.

We calculated the number of available adults for each family by adding up the number of adults under age 65 and then subtracting one half an adult if there are children under the age of six. Subtracting half an adult takes child-care needs into account.

When we compared the average number of available adults with the number of person-weeks actually worked by family members, we found that they were closely related. On average, for every additional working-age adult, a family adds about 30 weeks of paid labor per year.

The second factor affecting earnings is the average wage family members can obtain. This wage depends on the sex and age of paid workers in the family. In our sample, working men earned about twice as much as working women on a weekly basis. So, for example, even though single men and women worked almost identical numbers of weeks, the women earned far less than their male counterparts.

Maybe the next conservative proposal will be a national dating service.

Single mothers are burned on both accounts. They not only provide less paid labor than most other families, but also have no man in the family to bring in higher wages.

WHO'S WORKING NOW?

We also looked at which family members have been working more since the early 1970s. During this time, women have increased their participation in the paid labor force, while men have reduced theirs. Virtually all increases in average family earnings after 1973—among households with women—occurred because women worked more weeks per year.

Conservatives argue that tightening restrictions on welfare will spur the poor to work harder. But welfare cuts don't explain the heightened work effort by single mothers, who make up the main welfare population. *Moms* increased their work effort only between 1973 and 1979—before Congress enacted the major welfare cuts. Between 1979 and 1987, on the other hand, single mothers worked fewer hours.

In any case, changes in family work effort over the 1970s and 1980s made only a small dent in the earnings differences among family types. The large gaps wrought by disparate amounts of available adults and levels of wages dwarf the small changes in earnings over time. The earnings gap between *Ozzies* and *Moms* is narrowing, but at the current rate *Moms* will take 581 years to reach even half of what *Ozzies* earn.

SLICING THE INCOME PIE

The glaring inequalities in earnings between families would be less serious if other forms of income (property, alimony, child support, and government aid) offset those inequalities, but that isn't the case. Only *Elders* receive enough unearned income to raise their total income figure substantially.

Property income adds little to earnings, making up less than one-twelfth of the average family's income. Child support and alimony also barely affect total income, even for *Moms*, since two-thirds of single mothers receive no alimony/child support at all.

Government transfers such as Social Security and Aid to Families with Dependent Children (AFDC) represent the income source of last resort for families. The average family collects less than one-tenth of its income in transfers, but *Moms* and *Elders* benefit far more than average.

Although the government assists both single mothers and elders, the size of the public commitment diverges sharply between the two groups: elder households receive five times as much as single mothers. This doesn't mean the government guarantees the good life for elders, but it does mean that public assistance to single mothers is small indeed. What's more, overall government aid to single mothers fell steadily between 1973 and 1987 in real terms, while transfers to elders increased.

The changes in government transfers for these two types of family reflect the divergent paths of public policy toward people 65 and older versus single mothers. Policies that adjust the social-security program for inflation and secure stable funding demonstrate that society has a financial commitment to elders. But means-tested government programs, especially AFDC, have suffered from a conservative onslaught. Benefit levels have fallen: adjusted for inflation, the average monthly benefit for an AFDC recipient dropped from $150 in 1975 to $125 in 1987. Federal and state governments have tightened eligibility requirements and placed a whole new emphasis on the "responsibilities" of poor people who receive means-tested transfers.

The bottom line: Of *Elders* whose pre-transfer income left them below the poverty line, government aid lifted 75% out of poverty. Of *Moms* with poverty-level pre-transfer income, the government lifted only 10% out of poverty.

TIME FOR A DATING SERVICE

The evidence is clear: Some families have less income than others not because their work effort is inadequate, but because they lack the necessary available labor time and have access only to low-wage jobs.

As a result, cutting means-tested transfers has effects that Diane Dujon calls disastrous. "Instead of decreasing the burden on poor people," she declares, "they are adding to their burden." Welfare cuts will do little to make the poor work harder, because so many of the poor have little extra time to work. Even when work requirements are coupled with child care, single mothers don't stand to gain much, since the wages available to them are low. Over the 1970s and 1980s, welfare cuts have canceled out the small earnings gains single mothers made, leaving them with lower incomes than before.

In fairness to conservatives, they do look beyond hard work. They seek to assist single mothers by collecting child support from absent fathers—but we find that the amounts of income involved are very small. And conservatives call for single women to marry—which we find does make a big difference in family income. Maybe the next conservative proposal will be a national dating service for single mothers.

But women shouldn't be forced into marriage by poverty. An alternative is a concerted policy to reduce poverty by providing adequate government assistance. This *has* worked in the case of elders. Thus, the most direct way to reduce poverty is to increase government aid to the poor. Despite its political unpopularity, this policy makes sense—not just for elders, but across the board. ∎

RESOURCES: Albelda and Tilly, "Resources, Opportunity, and Effort" (working paper); Isabel Sawhill, "Poverty in the U.S.," *Journal of Economic Literature*, September 1988; Sheldon Danziger and Daniel Weinberg, *Fighting Poverty: What Works, What Doesn't*, 1980.

Dollars & Sense, May 1993

A Bad Bargain

*Why U.S. health care costs so much
and covers so few*

By Edie Rasell

The U.S. health care system is in crisis. Year by year, fewer people have insurance coverage, while costs skyrocket, draining vital resources from other critical social needs. Family budgets are squeezed and businesses are less competitive internationally.

Are we getting our money's worth from this enormous spending? No. Other countries spend much less to provide universal health insurance for their citizens—who also live longer and have fewer infant deaths. And despite years of concern and many "reforms," the U.S. situation is getting worse.

DENYING ACCESS

The number of uninsured is large and growing. In 1990, 36 million people, one out of every seven, had no health insurance. Since most people 65 years old and above are covered by Medicare, those under 65 are most at risk for being uninsured. Among the non-elderly, one out of six was uninsured in 1990. The percentage of people lacking coverage has been steadily rising over the past decade. Unfortunately, we lack consistent data on this trend, since after 1986 the federal government changed the main survey it uses to determine the number of uninsured.

Since many people periodically gain and lose their insurance, the number who are uninsured for some portion of a time period is much higher than that at any

one point in time. During the 28 months ending in February 1989, 61 million people—26% of the population—lacked coverage for at least one month.

Despite increases in Medicaid coverage, many of the poor lack insurance. Today Medicaid and other public programs cover only half of the poor, with a small percentage having private coverage, leaving 33% of them uninsured. Among the nonelderly, minorities are at greatest risk of being uninsured. Of whites, 13% are uninsured, while 23% of blacks, 35% of Hispanics, and 20% of other races lack health coverage.

Many people have no health coverage despite having regular jobs. More than half of the uninsured non-elderly either work full-time and year-round, or are family members of someone who does.

Fully 85% of the uninsured live in families where at least one member is employed.

WHY ARE SO MANY UNINSURED?

In all other industrialized nations, the government either provides universal health care coverage, or ensures that private-sector programs exist to cover essentially everyone. Why is the United States so different?

Except for Medicare and Medicaid, the U.S. government has left the responsibility to provide health insurance primarily to the private market. Insurance companies try to maximize profits by making coverage easily available to the generally healthy. Meanwhile, insurers deny coverage to, or make it more expensive for, the sick and those whom insurers think are more likely to become ill.

Relying on employers to provide health insurance leaves workers vulnerable. Many people feel, with good reason, that their coverage is insecure. Firms are free not to provide insurance, and if there is no union contract in the workplace, the firm can cancel its policy at any time. In 1990, 30% of full-time, year-round, never-unemployed workers aged 18-64 did *not* receive health insurance through their own employers.

Many policies do not cover "pre-existing conditions." If someone has an existing medical condition when they obtain a new insurance policy or enroll in a new

EDIE RASELL is a former family physician who currently is a health economist with the Economic Policy Institute in Washington, D.C.

IF YOU HAVE A CATASTROPHIC ILLNESS...

SUPREME COURT

... YOUR EMPLOYER CAN CUT YOUR HEALTH BENEFITS

WHAT KIND OF HEALTH INSURANCE IS THAT?!

IT'S A NEW PROGRAM WE CALL, "PAY AND PRAY"

WASSERMAN © '92 BOSTON GLOBE DIST. BY L.A.TIMES SYND.

Table 1: International health care spending, 1990

	Percent of GDP	$ per capita
Australia	7.5%	$1,151
Canada	9.0%	$1,795
France	8.9%	$1,379
Germany	8.1%	$1,287
Italy	7.7%	$1,138
Japan	6.5%	$1,145
Sweden	8.7%	$1,421
United Kingdom	6.2%	$932
United States	12.4%	$2,566

employer group plan, medical services related to this condition may not be covered initially. The exclusion period often lasts for three to 12 months, but may extend to the policy's lifetime. A 1987 survey found that 57% of all business firms had such exclusions in their policies.

If an employee's firm is self-insured (the firm pays employee health costs itself, without using an insurance company), as is the case for nearly half of all workers, then the company is free to modify its plan at any time to exclude previously covered services. For example, the courts have upheld the case of a Texas employer who reduced lifetime AIDS coverage from $1 million to $5,000 immediately after one employee was diagnosed with AIDS and filed his first claim.

Group policies cost less per person than do individual policies, and large group policies are cheaper than are those for small groups. One major reason for these cost differences is that insurers no longer spread health costs over all members of a community by combining some people's high costs with others' low costs, calculating an average, and then charging everyone the same moderately priced premium. Instead, insurers "cream skim," identifying low-cost people to insure and tempting them away from the larger group with the promise of cheaper premiums. This leaves most of the less healthy and more costly to insure in a group for which insurers charge rates that many people cannot afford.

Small group and individual policies also have higher administrative costs. For groups of fewer than 10 people, such costs are 35 to 40 cents of every dollar,

compared to six cents per dollar for large firms. In addition, insurers usually require that potential enrollees in small groups, or people seeking individual policies, have a physical exam and other tests to determine their probable need for future health care. If a doctor detects problems, insurers will boost premiums even higher, or deny coverage altogether. About 81 million people under age 65 have medical conditions that could lead insurance companies to raise premiums or refuse coverage if they sought to buy insurance as individuals or in small groups.

SKYROCKETING COSTS

Despite the declining rate of insurance coverage, national health care spending is rising rapidly. In 1992 we spent $839 billion for health care, or one-seventh of our Gross Domestic Product (GDP). Adjusted for inflation, spending rose by a whopping 8.5% over 1991, and by 39% since 1987. Over the past five years, the share of GDP devoted to health care has risen from 10.8% to 14%.

Health care spending is rising much faster than wages, business receipts, or government revenues. Thus health care is absorbing a growing share of the resources of individuals, firms, and the public sector. Many insurers are requiring people to pay rising portions of their health costs in various forms of cost-sharing, such as deductibles and co-payments. Between 1980 and 1991, the average cost of health insurance for an employee and family rose from $1,806 (in 1991 dollars) to $4,464, while employee out-of-pocket expenses for health care rose from $248 to $1,300.

The United States spends far more on health care than do other industrialized countries, despite having so many people uninsured (see Table 1). In 1990 U.S. per capita spending was nearly 1.5 times the level in Canada, the second highest spending country. Since other countries with lower spending have quite healthy populations and provide coverage for all their people, the United States could spend much less and still have universal, high-quality health care.

WHY COSTS ARE OUT OF CONTROL

There are two major reasons why the United States has greater spending than other countries—high charges by providers and intensive use of services.

Doctors, hospitals, and other medical providers in the United States charge more for medical care than abroad, and physicians earn much more than doctors in other countries (see Table 2).

In other industrialized countries, providers and insurers (or a government agency) negotiate fees and charges. The government's goal is to keep medical

Table 2: Average physician income, 1989

Canada (1988)	$81,679
Germany (1986)	86,704
Japan	45,324
United Kingdom	48,814
United States	155,800

Source: OECD Health Data, Organization for Economic Cooperation & Development, 1993.

charges in line with prices in the rest of the economy. In the United States, with the exceptions of Medicare and Medicaid, insurers' usual practice until recently was to pay physicians their "customary and reasonable" rate. This provides little check on price increases. Insurers also reimbursed hospitals based on whatever they charged, not for their actual costs to treat patients.

Part of the reason for high charges by U.S. care providers is huge administrative expenses, totalling 24% of all health spending. In contrast, for Canada's public-insurance system, which covers the entire population, administrative costs are

Table 3: Utilization of Services (annuals average per person)

	Hospital Days 1991	Physician Visits
Canada	2.0	6.6
France	2.8	7.1
Germany	3.3	11.5
Japan	4.0	12.9
United Kingdom	2.0	5.3
United States	1.2	5.3

Source: OECD Health Data, Organization for Economic Cooperation and Development, 1993.

only 11% of the total. Significantly, administrative costs in the U.S. Medicare system are in line with those in other countries. The U.S. Congress' General Accounting Office estimates that in 1991 we would have saved $67 billion if we had a single insurer, as in Canada.

Most of the administrative cost difference stems from the inefficiency of having over 1,500 private health insurance companies selling many different policies in the United States. Each policy may cover different services, restrict enrollees to particular doctors, and impose different levels of cost sharing, different deductibles, and different pe-existing condition exclusions. Administering all of this is an enormous paperwork burden for hospitals, doctors, and insurance companies.

But the most important reason costs in the United States surpass those elsewhere is our overuse of medical services. There are two ways to measure such use. One is *utilization*, which measures the frequency of encounters with the health care system—for example, the average number of doctor visits per person or number of days spent in hospitals. The second is *intensity* of use, which indicates the number and type of services received when someone does visit a doctor or hospital. While high utilization is not a problem in the United States, intensity is the major reason U.S. health care costs surpass those elsewhere.

Compared to other countries, Americans have quite low utilization rates, as shown in Table 3. We average far fewer days in the hospital than do people in any other industrialized country. Visits to the doctor are also less frequent than in other nations.

Policy-makers and analysts often pro-

pose increased cost sharing as a way to discourage utilization and reduce the national health care bill. But since we do not have excessive utilization, this is misguided policy. Forcing further cuts in utilization will only reduce access to necessary care.

In contrast, the intensity of services used in the United States far surpasses levels in other industrialized countries. Americans do not go to the doctor or enter the hospital very often, but when we do, we receive excessive services compared to people elsewhere.

Intensity of use is high in the United States for several reasons. We have relatively fewer primary-care doctors, and more specialists, than other nations. Specialists tend to order more tests and do more medical procedures. Second, for decades our health care system has rewarded physicians in the United States for "doing" rather than thinking. Payments by insurers for procedures and tests are far higher than for equivalent amounts of time and levels of skill devoted to physical examinations, thinking about solutions to medical problems, talking to patients, or "just" prescribing medicines.

Some doctors who have financial interests in laboratories or radiology facilities order far more tests than those with-

out similar investments. A study of laboratories in Florida, for example, found that those owned by physicians did twice as many tests per patient as did laboratories owned by non-physicians. Another study found that doctors with financial interests in radiology facilities referred patients for x-rays four times more often than did physicians who had not invested in such facilities.

Excess medical equipment and facilities drive up costs in two ways. First, because machines are plentiful, doctors are encouraged to do too many tests. This raises the national health care bill and causes needless pain and suffering. Second, if there are too many machines, then even after doing excessive numbers of tests, the machines are still under-used. For the equipment's owner to recover its purchase price, the charge for each test must be higher than if the machine were fully utilized.

Another factor that contributes to the high testing rate is the U.S. medical "culture" and the standard of practice taught in medical schools. Many doctors' philosophy is to do everything possible for the patient, to do every test no matter how slim the chance that it will provide useful information. The result is that doctors perform many unnecessary and inappropriate procedures. Several studies reported in medical journals have examined surgical procedures to determine whether they were necessary ("appropriate"), possibly needed ("equivocal"), or unnecessary ("inappropriate"). As Table 4 shows, physicians performed 14% to 32% of selected heart, neck, and stomach procedures for inappropriate reasons, and an additional 9% to 36% were equivocal.

Physicians' practice "style" and local standards of care have a large impact on intensity of use and on medical costs. One recent study examined services pro-

Table 4: Running up the tab—unnecessary operations

Operation	Appropriate	Equivocal	Inappropriate
coronary angiography	74%	9%	17%
carotid endarterectomy	35%	32%	32%
endoscopy	72%	11%	17%
coronary artery bypasses	56%	30%	14%
pacemaker insertion	44%	36%	20%

vided by doctors to elderly patients in over 300 metropolitan areas. Researchers adjusted for differences between areas in the seriousness of patients' illnesses, and for other factors that influence the need for medical services. Despite these adjustments, differences in the amounts and types of services provided to patients in these cities still resulted in a two-fold difference in spending per patient. Moreover, in those cities where doctors provided more services and costs were higher, patients' health after treatment was no better.

There are several other factors that contribute to our high and rising spending, such as malpractice suits, drug-industry profits, experimental treatments, and the aging of the population. But in contrast to claims made by some medical-care analysts, these factors are only responsible for a small portion of our high and rising expenditures.

Malpractice suits, and physicians' resulting tendency to practice "defensive medicine," contribute to the high intensity of use, but this problem only increases national health spending by about 2%-3%. Population aging is not now a major cost factor, but it will become more significant over the next few decades.

The lack of preventive services, such as prenatal care, immunizations, treatment for infectious diseases, and some preventive screening measures such as Pap smears, raises costs and causes unnecessary suffering. The expense of treating illnesses that may occur without preventive care is greater than the costs of prevention.

Another issue is "cost shifting," which occurs when one payer—an insurance company, a business firm, the government, or an individual—shifts costs to another payer. For example, in both the Medicare and Medicaid programs the government sets payment rates for hospitals. Currently Medicare rates cover only about 90% of patients' actual hospital costs, and Medicaid rates cover only 80%. To avoid losing money, hospitals make up for their losses on Medicare, Medicaid, and uncompensated care (care for which hospitals receive no payments) by charging other payers more. This shift increases private insurers' payments by 28%, according to the Prospective Pay-

ment Assessment Commission, an agency established by Congress to make recommendations about Medicare payments to physicians.

By competing to obtain lower rates from hospitals, insurance companies cause cost shifts among themselves. An insurer with many local policyholders may negotiate "discounts" from hospitals. In return for the insurer designating a particular hospital as an approved site for its enrollees, the hospital must charge them lower rates. Hospitals pass the differences between the discounted rates and their true costs onto patients covered by other insurance companies.

Cost shifting can reduce total costs for

a particular insurer, but it does not reduce the *national* health care bill. Some analysts argue that cost shifting actually raises spending. To the extent one payer can shift costs onto another payer (including onto individuals by raising their copayments and deductibles), this reduces the incentive for concerted action to truly control national spending. Cost shifting is, however, only a minor factor in the overall cost spiral.

BUT ARE WE HEALTHY?

Despite spending more on health care than other industrialized countries, we are not proportionally more healthy. Life expectancy at birth for U.S. females is below the level in 17 other countries, and the rate for men is lower than in 21 other nations. Twenty-two countries, including Italy, Spain, Hong Kong, and Singapore, have a lower infant mortality rate than the United States.

These measures of health depend on more than the health care system. Pov-

erty and the factors that often accompany it, including a poor diet stress, and dangerous environmental and occupational exposures, all worsen average health in the United States. The lack of prenatal care is a major contributing factor to high infant mortality. The U.S. child immunization rate is lower than in many Third World countries, and has been falling recently.

Compared to other nations, the United States has an abundance of high-technology medical equipment and facilities, but we impose needless pain and suffering by doing too many tests and procedures. We have too many specialists and too few primary-care physicians. We

---

The United States has helicopter transport to ultra-sophisticated trauma units, but little transportation to help rural and inner-city residents reach their family doctors.

---

have helicopter transport to ultra-sophisticated trauma units, but little transportation to help rural or inner-city residents reach their family doctors.

The quality of American medical care can be the best in the world, but it also can be very bad. The United States needs a fundamental overhaul of the financing and delivery of health care. We must address the escalating costs, lack of access, and uneven quality of care. And we must remember that a society with high levels of poverty and unemployment can never be a healthy society. ■

Resources: Rashi Fein, "National Health Insurance: Telling the Good from the Bad," *Dissent*, Spring 1992; Robert G. Evans, "Tension, Compression and Sheer: Directions, Stresses, and Outcomes of Health Care Cost Control," *Journal of Health Politics, Policy and Law*, 1990, 15(1); Thomas Bodenheimer, "Should We Abolish the Private Health Insurance Industry?," *International Journal of Health Services*, 1990, 20(2).

Dollars & Sense, October 1989

Natural Enemies

*Private profits, public interests
at war over the environment*

By Patricia Horn

A sign two blocks from the Jersey City, New Jersey, city hall reads, "This area contains dangerous and contaminated materials that are harmful to human life." A chromium refinery that once occupied the lot contaminated the soil with 46 times the amount of carcinogens that New Jersey deems safe.

In the 16th century, Juan Rodriguez Cabrillo sailed into what is now the bay of Los Angeles and christened it Bahia de los Fumos—Bay of Smoke. Today, the smog capital of America more than lives up to that name. For 176 days last year, the ozone in L.A.'s air exceeded federal standards.

This March, the Exxon Valdez hit a reef, and 11 million gallons of crude oil poured into Alaska's Prince William Sound, saturating birds' wings with oil, clogging fish's gills, and spoiling hundreds of miles of coastline. The magnitude of that disaster stands out, but similar events happen every day. Last year, the Coast Guard counted some 5,000 oil and other toxic spills in U.S. waters.

For at least 20 years, our national awareness of the link between pollution and survival has grown with each new crisis—oil spills, dying lakes, contaminated water, overflowing garbage, toxic dumps, and global warming. But despite this Sword of Damocles dangling over us, we have barely begun to provide solutions.

The fact is that our private enterprise economy severely restricts progress against pollution. We rely on private decisions of individual firms to determine the course of our economy. Operating individually, these firms make the investment and production decisions that are best for their own profits, and those decisions often conflict with what would be best for the environment. Operating together, these firms push government policies that encourage growth, frequently at the expense of the air, land, or water.

The fight against pollution is ultimately a fight to restrict and change the private enterprise system. It requires the government to intervene more actively in the economy and citizens to exert pressure on private firms.

HOSTAGES TO GROWTH

Capitalism needs growth. The expansion of economic activity creates new markets, products, and technologies that make it possible for businesses to make profits. One of the marvels of capitalism is that, when it works well and each individual firm pursues opportunities in its own niche, the resulting investments lead the whole system to expand. This overall expansion, in turn, creates more opportunities and what the system needs: growth.

According to business leaders and government officials, we all have an interest in economic growth, and therefore in letting business go its way with a minimum of restrictions. Growth means more jobs, higher incomes, and more goods and services. When there are no other options, this is a hard argument to counter.

But growth, it turns out, often involves environmental destruction. When we hand businesses the bill for this destruction, they reply with the specter of stag-nation and recession: unemployment, bankrupt companies, and higher prices. Given the present economic system, the threat is real. Kentucky miners have good reason to fear that strict emission standards on coal-fired generators will cost them jobs. Consumers know their electric bills will be even higher if utilities are fully prevented from polluting.

The favorite yardstick of economic welfare and economic progress, gross national product (GNP), reflects capitalism's bias, measuring the aggregate value only of the things that are produced and sold in the market. The GNP measure distorts the picture of what is happening to the economy, exaggerating economic growth and ignoring environmental degradation. It fails to take account of the costs of foul air, for example, or of unclean lakes, rivers, and oceans.

These are costs for which no money changes hands, but they are real nonetheless. The quality of our lives diminishes when smog suffocates us and waters are despoiled. Our future economic welfare is also diminished because these acts make future production more difficult and costly. Thus the growth registered by GNP is in many ways illusory.

What if the GNP took account of these social costs? Certainly the U.S. GNP would grow more slowly, if at all. Economist and futurist Hazel Henderson has pointed out that if we do not measure "the social costs of a polluted environment, disrupted communities, disrupted family life...[then] we have no idea whether we are going forward or backwards."

THE EXTERNAL WORLD

When a private firm makes decisions, it only takes into consideration the costs it actually incurs and the income it actually receives. When one firm's decision forces another person or firm to incur costs, those costs have no place in its profit calculations.

Occasionally, a firm's actions confer benefits on others. A classic example of a positive external effect—or positive "externality"—is the case of a honey farm. Farmers raise bees to produce honey and sell it for a profit. In the process, however, anyone who has an orchard or flower garden in the vicinity will benefit without

PATRICIA HORN is an editor at *Dollars & Sense*.

fighting to block the cleanup by arguing that the cost will be much higher.

FEDERAL FAILURES

In recent years, the environmental crisis has worsened to the point where no one can ignore it. In the United States, the hidden costs of profit-driven growth are even higher than in other countries because government regulation and planning are so limited. Even staunch conservatives have finally begun to call for action, but their programs are still mired in reverence for the free market and minimal government involvement.

This June, in a shift from Ronald Reagan's denial of the connection between coal-plant pollution and acid rain, George Bush asked Congress to strengthen the 1970 Clean Air Act. Not surprisingly, Bush's rhetoric went far beyond what the proposal actually provides. Bush's promise that sulfur dioxide emissions would be reduced by 10 million tons is achieved in the bill only by counting some reductions that have already taken place. The bill would actually allow an increase of nitrous oxide emissions over present levels. The changes are touted as a "reduction," however, because they would be less than the amount that would be emitted in the future under present regulation.

Beyond its accounting shortcomings, the real problem with the Bush proposal lies in its basic approach. Firms would be allowed a certain level of emissions, and those firms that achieve lower levels than this standard could sell their "right" to pollute to other firms. So one coal-burning electric utility could emit more pollutants if another, cleaner plant offsets the excess. Allowing companies to buy and sell the right to pollute would supposedly promote economic efficiency. They would pollute the most where doing so brought the biggest profit payoff. Such is the world of the free market.

Even on its own terms, the Bush plan is set up to fail. The problems of enforcement by an underfunded Environmental Protection Agency, for example, are immense. Each firm's pollution levels would have to be checked against its purchases and sales of the right to pollute. Numerous loopholes make it likely that firms will find legal ways to avoid the bill's restrictions.

having to pay for the bees' pollination tasks.

It is far easier to come up with examples of negative externalities, and many go by the more common name of pollution. When an Ohio utility burns coal to generate electricity, it emits sulfur dioxide and nitrous oxides. As a consequence, acid rain falls on the Northeast and Canada, killing animal life in lakes and rivers, ruining trees, and slowly dissolving buildings and statues. The tourism, fishing, and logging industries suffer, but the utility doesn't bear the costs.

Traditional economic theory, rooted in 19th century optimism and the exploitation of vast colonial resources, treats such negative externalities as relatively rare events. In 20th century reality, however, negative externalities dominate our lives.

In each case, the owners of the polluting company do not pay for the abuse of the environment, the damage to human health, and the drain on public resources caused by their activities. So they don't take account of those costs. If they were forced to pay the true social costs, they would certainly cut back their operations.

If the polluters themselves do not pay, someone else does—through poor health and higher health bills, increased taxes to pay for clean-up, more personal expenses such as bottled water and air filters, higher prices in other industries, and the incalculable cost of a less pleasant world in which to live.

The part of the pollution bill that we can readily measure is growing rapidly. In Los Angeles, for instance, air-quality authorities estimate that the health cost of smog in the region is $3.65 billion every year, while California agriculture suffers to the tune of $7 billion. An 18-year cleanup currently under consideration for L.A. carries an officially estimated price tag of $2.8 billion for the first five years—a bargain from a social standpoint. Industry in the city, with its eyes narrowly focused on current profits, is

While the Bush plan may have some impact on air pollution, it cannot work because it attempts to control rather than prevent pollution. The distinction between the two is critical, as Barry Commoner pointed out in a 1987 *New Yorker* article. Control allows pollutants to be produced but blocks them from entering the air, water, or ground. Prevention stops their production outright. To illustrate the effectiveness of prevention, Commoner cited the 1972 U.S. ban on DDT and related insecticides. By 1983, the average DDT levels in human body fat had fallen 71%.

Efforts aimed at only controlling pollution have been less successful. To reduce carbon-monoxide pollution, the

A small first step would be to establish a better way of assessing our economic progress. The GNP measure gives a high value to private benefits and downplays social costs that are external to the market. In fact, alternative measures of growth are available. Though they are imperfect, many are better than what we use now.

The World Resources Institute, for example, has suggested a measure that would deduct the depletion of resources from any year's GNP. In its 1989 study, *Wasting Assets*, the Institute applies this yardstick to Indonesia. Measured the traditional way, Indonesia's GNP rose an average of 7.1% per year from 1971 to 1984. When the depreciation of only

Unless the corporate-minded Interior Department files an appeal, the court's decision could add billions to the bills that Exxon and other polluters now face. While the enormous costs may bankrupt even the biggest firm, they could also force potential polluters to think twice—or thrice—before engaging in ecological madness.

Reducing pollution is one part of a solution, but it does not eliminate capitalism's growth imperative. Nor does it eliminate the conflict between jobs and the environment. Another necessary step is assigning the public sector a more active, more overt role in determining industry policy. National and regional planning is necessary to direct investment toward long-term development that preserves, rather than destroys, the environment. Moreover, only through public action can we provide an adequate number of jobs, assuring people that protecting the environment does not mean they will be left out in the cold.

Finally, if planning is left to the state, we must also change whom the state represents. To do so requires the continual building and rebuilding of a democratic, popular movement. Such a movement must counterbalance the power of private business, but also counterbalance the state itself. Experience in the Soviet Union and other centrally planned economies demonstrates that the government, when driven solely by a growth imperative and not controlled by a popular movement, can abuse the environment as badly as can private firms.

The fight against pollution is ultimately a fight to restrict and change the private enterprise system.

---

federal government requires car makers to install emissions-control devices in automobiles. But between 1975 and 1985, such emissions fell a scant 14%, and the emission level was again rising at the end of this period. As Commoner concludes, "The few real improvements have been achieved not by adding control devices or concealing pollutants (as by pumping hazardous wastes into deep water-bearing strata), but simply by eliminating pollutants."

Of course, the goal of eliminating carbon-monoxide pollution will be elusive as long as we rely on the internal-combustion engine for transportation. Huge investments in public transportation would be essential to any program aimed at preventing auto-originating pollution. But this solution falls outside the scope of the free market.

TOWARD A CLEANER FUTURE

We do, of course, need to provide for our economic well-being. People need goods and services, and people need jobs. So how do we go about using nature's gifts wisely?

three of the nation's major resources are subtracted, that figure falls to 4.0%. And Indonesia's domestic investment, a prerequisite for economic development and long-term growth, is actually negative in some years if the costs of depletion are deducted. Many industrialized countries—among them Japan, France, Germany, and Norway—have similar measures that account for environmental destruction.

Of course, an alternative measure of economic activity by itself will not ensure a clean environment. Changing corporate behavior requires organized pressure. Indeed, a citizen movement to force capitalists to fully absorb the cost of their pollution is emerging. As of this summer, the movement has had some success in court. In July, a Washington, D.C., federal appeals court overturned government regulations and ruled unanimously that polluters must pay to restore the environment to its original condition: "From the bald eagle to the blue whale and snail darter, natural resources have values that are not fully captured by the market system," the court proclaimed.

A public industrial policy to manage the economy and the environment will require giving environmentalists, workers, and citizens a role in investment decisions. As Commoner has written, "Economics and environmental gains can be achieved only if the social need for both environmental quality and economic growth is allowed to govern the choices of product technology." ■

RESOURCES: Barry Commoner, *Poverty of Power* and "A Reporter at Large: The Environment," *New Yorker*, June 1987; Robert Repetto, et al., *Wasting Assets: Natural Resources in the National Income Accounts*, World Resources Institute; James Robertson with Andre Carothers, "The New Economics: Accounting for a Healthy Planet," *Greenpeace*, January/February 1989.

Dollars & Sense, December 1991

Left in the Dust

*U.S. trails other nations in
support for the poor*

By Randy Albelda

The United States had steadier growth and lower unemployment during the 1980s than any European industrialized country except Sweden. Nevertheless, by the middle of the 1980s, the U.S. poverty rate was double that of every industrialized European nation except the United Kingdom.

A new study by the Joint Center for Political and Economic Studies, an African-American managed think tank in Washington, D.C., attributes this contrast to differences in tax policies and social programs. Years of regressive U.S. tax policies and underfunded social programs have taken their toll. While poverty has also grown in Western Europe, more progressive tax policies and more generous income transfer programs have diminished its severity.

In 1986, the study found, U.S. policies added to the number of America's poor. That is, taxes pushed more people into poverty than income transfer programs pulled out. Surveying 8,000 households, researchers accounted for taxes paid, as well as cash and "near-cash" benefits that added to household income, such as unemployment compensation, disability, food stamps, and Aid for Families with Dependent Children. Instead of decreasing the number of poor households, the combination of regressive taxes and inadequate social benefits increased the number of households living in poverty.

In contrast, in the United Kingdom that year, almost half of the households which were poor before subtracting taxes and adding public benefits were no longer poor after paying taxes and receiving income transfers. The Center's Katherine McFate, who coordinated the project along with William Julius Wilson of the University of Chicago and Roger Lawson of England's University of Southampton, points to paid parental leave policies and child allowances as two examples of social programs common in Europe but not in the United States. McFate also notes that a great proportion of America's unemployed receive no unemployment benefits.

The study highlights differences in public attitudes toward taxation and social programs between the United States and Europe. Here, the public views taxes as means to pay for public services. Europeans, however, demonstrate greater commitment to leveling income inequality and ensuring that no one falls too far below a national income norm, McFate comments. Despite the spread of conservatism in Europe, and despite the economic difficulties European nations have had, both tax and income-transfer policies still serve these goals.

"The United States stands in ignominious isolation," the report charges. "Among industrialized countries, the United States has the highest incidence of poverty among the non-elderly and the widest distribution of poverty across all age and family groups." It is also "the only western democracy that has failed to give a significant portion of its poor a measure of income security."

POOR SHOWING

Researchers compared poverty and social policies in the United States, Canada, France, West Germany, Italy, the Netherlands, Sweden, and the United Kingdom. To compare across countries, they defined a family as poor if its income was half or less of the country's median family income. The official U.S. poverty line is lower than this standard, so the poverty rates reported by JCPES are higher than official U.S. rates. Researchers only studied families headed by someone 20 to 55 years of age.

Researchers found that poverty grew in the early and mid-eighties in every country except France, where the poverty rate stayed the same, and the Netherlands, where it dropped slightly. While family-related changes such as divorce caused some of the increases in poverty, job loss and wage drops were the most common causes. By 1986, 18% of U.S. households and 12.5% of British households studied were poor. The following year, about 14% of Canadians studied were poor, compared to fewer than 8% in the Netherlands and 9% in Sweden.

By using a combination of tax policies and social programs, every country except the United States pulled at least one-fifth of its poor citizens out of poverty during the years studied. (Due to data-collection problems, researchers sampled different years in different countries.) In 1979, government action lifted less than 1% of poor U.S. families studied out of poverty, compared to 33% in the United Kingdom.

KINDER AND GENTLER?
TRY DEEPER AND NASTIER

Not only were more U.S. households poor compared to other countries, but Americans were more likely to be "severely" poor. In Europe and Canada, household incomes hovered close to the median national income. In the United States, more households fell far below the national median.

Researchers also found that the poor in the United States stayed poor longer than poor families elsewhere. More than 14% of all families with children stayed poor for three years in a row. In contrast, 12% in Canada and less than 2% in West Germany, France, and the Netherlands remained poor for three years or more.

Researchers compared poverty rates for blacks in the United States to foreign-born people in West Germany (mostly

RANDY ALBELDA, a member of the *Dollars & Sense* Collective, teaches economics at the University of Massachusetts-Boston.

Turks), many of whom work in low-status industrial jobs. They found that both Turks in West Germany and blacks in the United States were three times more likely to be poor than whites living in the same country. But because U.S. poverty rates were so high, white Americans were about as likely to be poor as were Turks in West Germany. In other words, the poverty rate for Turks in West Germany was only slightly higher than the rate for white Americans—18% for Turks and 15% for U.S. whites. (U.S. blacks faced a staggering 50% poverty rate.)

Even more revealing, almost half of African Americans who experienced poverty stayed poor for three years or more, compared to less than 10% of U.S. whites and only 4% of Turks and other foreign-born families in West Germany.

TREAT YOUR CHILDREN WELL?

Poverty rates for single-parent families were particularly high in the United States, Canada, and the United Kingdom. In each of these countries, such families experienced poverty about three times more often than families headed by married couples. This contrasts markedly with other countries studied, which had lower poverty rates for all families and less difference in rates between single-parent and couple-headed families.

Researchers attributed the success of these countries in ameliorating the financial burden of single parenthood to "the combined effects of advance child-support payments, relatively generous income 'support' packages for families with children in general, and support services—particularly publicly funded child care—that allow mothers to remain in the labor force during their child-rearing years."

Sweden succeeded in attaining the lowest poverty rates for both single-parent and couple-headed families. Far more Swedish mothers from both family types worked than in any other country, though most single parents worked only part-time. At the same time, almost all single parents relied on government programs for support. National commitments to full employment, progress in gender pay equity, collection of child-support payments, and publicly supported child care combined to give single mothers a greater measure of income security

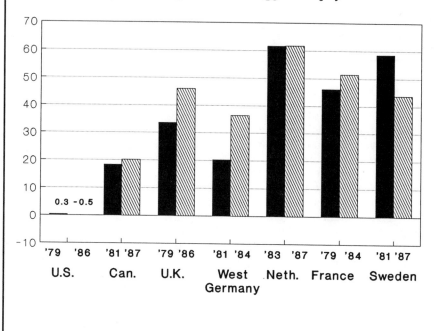

Out of poverty
Percent of originally poor households lifted out of poverty by government programs after accounting for tax payments

than in any other nation.

In fact, Sweden's generous child allowances help lift over 80% of poor mothers and their families out of poverty, while U.S. social policies (mostly tax credits for working mothers and Aid to Families with Dependent Children) lift fewer than 5% of poor female-headed families out of poverty.

TARNISHED MODEL

The report concludes that continental European countries have a variety of family-assistance programs that, if copied in the United States, could improve the lives of many Americans. McFate says the jury is still out on whether the United States will go in the direction of its generous European counterparts, or whether European nations will follow the conservative U.S. lead. Despite Britain's "progress" in "catching up" with U.S. poverty rates, many European family-assistance programs have survived the recent spread of conservatism. On this side of the Atlantic, McFate notes that congressional representatives recently intro-

duced several pieces of child-credit and parental-leave legislation.

The U.S. experience has undoubtedly contributed to Europe's rightward shift, in part because the U.S. economy shone in comparison to Europe in the early 1980s. But today, Europeans are less eager to endorse U.S. economic policies. "America," comments McFate, "is looking kind of tarnished as a model."

This perception was borne out, according to McFate, by European researchers who visited Washington, D.C., during the study. Many of them had not visited this country for several years, and the number of people begging on the streets, McFate says, appalled the European researchers. ■

RESOURCE: *Poverty, Inequality and the Crisis of Social Policy: Public Policy Challenges in a New World Order* is available from the Joint Center for Political and Economic Studies, 1301 Pennsylvania Avenue N.W., Suite 400, Washington, D.C., 20004-1797.

The Global Economy

Dollars & Sense, December 1991

A Market: But What Kind?

*Four views on the future
of the post-Soviet economy*

Esther Kingston-Mann, *a Soviet history professor at the University of Massachusetts at Boston,* **John Feffer**, *an associate editor at the* **World Policy Journal**, *and* **Jeanine Braithwaite**, *a professor of Soviet economics at Kalamazoo College in Michigan, wrote their responses.*

We received these comments in October. By the time this article reaches you in December, the Soviet Union may look very different. The rapid pace of change and disintegration made deciding on terms difficult. In most instances, we used the word "Soviet" in reference to its people. We call the area the Soviet Union, though we recognize that it is not one nation.

The attempted coup in the Soviet Union in August sparked a new urgency among Soviets to settle on a plan to rescue their collapsing economy. But in the aftermath of the coup, the future of the republics remains unclear. Much of the confusion centers on the unsettled political scene, but deeper questions revolve around the nature of the economy.

Newspapers, magazines, and the electronic media have presented us with a skewed picture of the debate among the Soviets and the likely impact of proposed changes. Blinded by the rhetoric of free markets and democracy, most Western reporters focus on those who champion the free market wholeheartedly, or zero in on Communist Party officials desperately clinging to power. Yet the range of opinion in the post-Soviet Union is far more diverse than those two polarities. There **are** other voices of change.

In particular, the Soviet Union has an active trade union movement whose members have diverse views on the shape of the future economy. With almost all Soviet workers belonging to a union, trade unions have played an important role in the economy. Soviet trade unions differ greatly from U.S. unions. In the past they rarely struck against the state or management. Their main task was to administer the extensive Soviet social security system of health care, child care, cultural clubs, and sports facilities at the workplace. Party-dominated trade unions also ensured compliance with state labor legislation, safety and hygiene standards, and represented workers in yearly collective agreement negotiations.

But **perestroika** and **glasnost** changed that. Since 1989, workers in a number of republics have demanded a voice in managing factories and unions. They have struck for a wide range of political and economic demands. But the role unions may have in shaping the economy has gone largely unnoticed in the West. So, too, have numerous other developments that run counter to the myth of a free market.

Following are four views on the future of the post-Soviet economy. We asked each respondent to comment on the Union's economic future and the possibilities for democratic progressive change. **Dollars & Sense** Staff Editor **Patricia Horn** interviewed four Soviet trade unionists traveling in the United States.

ESTHER KINGSTON-MANN

Professor of Soviet History
University of Massachusetts at Boston

Within the Soviet Union, the future of the economy and the government is being debated at every level of society. Although some similar themes are being raised by intellectuals and by miners and factory workers, intellectuals have not played a significant role in the labor unrest and strike activity that have erupted since the advent of *perestroika* and *glasnost*.

While Western commentators have tended to focus either on the advocates of an unrestricted free market or on those who demand a return to Stalinist-style protection and control, there are Soviet economists and sociologists who fall into neither of these categories. Favoring a measure of market reform, these intellectuals and activists argue as well that markets alone cannot create a healthy economy. Among this group, Tatiana Zaslavskaia is one of the most interesting. An economic sociologist who was for many years president of the So-

Soviet society has failed to provide real opportunities for citizens to fulfill their needs, talents, and preferences.

viet Sociological Association, she is seen by many as the real author of *perestroika*. In the early 1980s, Zaslavskaia presented a paper at a secret seminar in Moscow on the sociological bases of economic growth and decline. This paper, which linked the low level of labor incentive in the Soviet Union to the pervasiveness of Party privileges and corruption in the workplace, circulated underground for years and served to establish some of the basic principles of the ensuing *perestroika* debate. A supporter of Gorbachev since the mid-1980s, Zaslavskaia was asked to be a member of his Presidential Council in 1990.

According to Zaslavskaia, Soviet society has failed to provide real opportunities for its citizens to fulfill their needs, talents, and preferences; workers have had no reason to believe that the material rewards they received were a product of their "individual knowledge, abilities, and will" rather than party connections and privileges. As she sees it, the desire to work has been weakened and undermined by empty promises of equality and a worker's sense of powerlessness to effect change. Economists and sociologists like Zaslavskaia have argued that in addition to the incentives provided by new rights of property ownership, a measure of workplace democracy on the shop floor and in the boardroom of factories, laboratories, and research institutes will encourage labor initiative.

Below the level of policy-makers, scholars, and politicians, workers debate similar issues. In recent years, the demands of strikers in various regions of the Soviet Union have gone far beyond the issue of wages. In the Donetsk mining region of the Ukraine, miners have been engaged in a variety of strike activities since 1989. In all of them, workers demanded an end to what they described as a stagnant system ruled by inefficient and corrupt Party functionaries who were contemptuous of workers. Most Donetsk labor leaders seem to have placed their hopes on market-style reform as a corrective to the inequities of the past. Interviews recently conducted with leaders of the March/April 1991 Donetsk City Strike Committee revealed not only a willingness to accept wage inequality based on skills or the numbers of hours worked, but an extremely idealized view of an American-style market economy. They assume, for example, that American unions are immensely powerful institutions. They presume that in market economies, unions can defend the rights of workers and prevent employers from laying off employees and from hiring non-union workers or strike breakers.

But half of the Donetsk miners did not go out on strike in 1991. Among some of the workers who struck in 1989 but not in 1991, recent experiences suggested different lessons and perspectives. At the Kuibyshev mine, the 1989 strike led workers to establish a Council of Labor Collectives for the Donetsk coal mining district. This democratically elected council has improved working conditions for its members. In 1991, the mine turned a profit for the first time in decades. Workers instituted a profit-sharing plan and, since 1989, have seen their wages triple. Like their counterparts in the Donetsk City Strike Committee, council leaders assume the existence of a very powerful labor movement in the present and future.

But they disagree on wage inequality. When the leaders of the Council on Labor Collectives recently proposed a contract for the mine director that would allow his income to be triple a miner's wage, their members erupted in anger and hostility.

As winter approaches, the economic tensions across the country may well reach a breaking point. If supplies of food and clothing continue to dwindle, and the unemployment "normal" to free market (but not to Soviet) economics begins to skyrocket, a second and much more powerful coup attempt may take place, in which Stalinists will assume the mantle of sole protector of labor. Given the external pressures for privatization, neither labor activists nor economic sociologists like Zaslavskaia may be able to generate alternatives that will save the post-Soviet Union from a choice between the Stalinists and a market-driven "survival of the fittest."

SOVIET TRADE UNIONISTS

Vitaly Golovatchev, *member of the* **Trud** *editorial board, the main Soviet trade union newspaper;* **Tatiana Rogova,** *International Department of General Confederation of Trade Unions;* **Talkun Sabitor,** *President, Agroindustrial Complex Workers Union;* **Peter Serdyuk,** *President of Chernigov Regional Federation of Trade Unions. This commentary is an edited version of an interview with all four unionists by* **D&S** *Staff Editor Patricia Horn. The opinions expressed here are just some of many perspectives held by unionists in the Soviet Union.*

Within the labor movement, our only agreement is that in a market economy the working person should be protected. The trade unions, at this particular time, disagree with the government and the parliament about the conversion to a market because there are no guarantees about living standards, wages, or employment opportunities. Trade unions are more cautious than people in the parliament.

We are concerned about the breakup of the Soviet Union because if the republics disassociate, we won't be able to protect workers. The supply of raw materials, production, and spare parts connect enterprises in different republics. Without these relationships, industry will collapse.

The priority for trade unions right now is to help people live through this difficult period. Living conditions have deteriorated for many people. About one-third of the population now lives close to the poverty line. That is too many. The main challenge for us is to care for those who find themselves below the poverty line.

How much is required for minimum living? In previous years, we did not examine living standards, or what the minimum living standard should be. We are now doing these calculations.

The deteriorating economy and deteriorating production prevent us from increasing wages. We must be concerned with increasing labor efficiency. We are searching for new ways to accelerate development of the country, such as converting from military to civilian production.

We still believe that major industries should remain state-owned. They should not be privatized. It is easier for workers in major industries to protect their rights in a centralized economy.

JOHN FEFFER

Associate editor of **World Policy Journal** *at the New School for Social Research, New York.*

If we want to know the economic future of the Soviet Union, we should simply look to the present travails of Eastern Europe: recession, unemployment, inflation, growing disparities in wealth. Although proof of the pain of overnight capitalism lies scant miles to the west, the post-Soviet Union is nonetheless on a trajectory toward market-oriented shock therapy, with few alternative routes in sight.

The independent Socialist party has but marginal support. The Social Democratic party and the independent trade union movement (the Confederation of Working People, not the Communist-dominated United Front of Working People) make no bones about their market fancies, however vague they are. The weak federal leadership as well as the radical democrats, nationalists and former Communists governing in the republics are all, to one degree or another, bracing for shock therapy. Every powerful international interest, from the U.S. government and Harvard University to the International Monetary Fund and the Group of Seven (the world's leading industrialized countries), urges laissez-faire *tout de suite.*

But won't the oft-quoted egalitarianism of the average post-Soviet citizen disrupt this cozy consensus? True, according to many polls, the average working Ivan favors neither large disparities in income, the removal of the social net, nor belt-tightening and endless austerity. Unfortunately, egalitarianism is a fickle value. In Poland, for instance, the population seemed similarly poised to reject free-market solutions in the first Solidarity period (1980-81) only to reverse their sympathies by 1989. The Czech and Slovak population, immediately after their velvet revolution, overwhelmingly rejected overnight capitalism according to several polls. Yet they, too, reversed their position when domestic technocrats and Western advisers set to work selling capitalism.

Who then can stand up to the promoters of an idealized market, and what can they offer as alternatives? Anything resembling Yugoslav-style self-management or democratic planning or ecologically sound communitarian development is bound to fail in the short term, not because these options are theoretically deficient, but because the international economic community would simply not countenance them.

Combining one part pragmatism with one part idealism, I believe the most compelling progressive alternative for the Soviet Union is a democratic industrial policy. A state-sponsored policy would modernize potentially successful enterprises and encourage "infant" industries. Independent unions, governments, and emerging business associations would negotiate federal, confederate, or republic economic policy. Private farmers and those who voluntarily remain in cooperatives would negotiate price supports with the governments and, one can only hope, benefit from an internationally funded revamping of regional distribution. Unions would agree to a certain degree of austerity in exchange for guaranteed retraining programs and unemployment benefits. The government would abandon its laissez-faire notion of the market and its exclusive control over fiscal and monetary policy but gain from the stability born of social consensus.

Given the region's present disarray, an industrial policy for the post-Soviet Union would at first be only a rough negotiating framework among workers, employers, and the states—a roundtable comparable to those that spread through Eastern Europe in 1989-90.

To present a clear alternative to center and right-wing parties, a strong labor movement and the Social Democratic party must both champion such a policy. If the party doesn't, social democracy will fail at the polls as surely as it did in the Eastern European elections of 1990-91.

JEANINE BRAITHWAITE

Professor of Soviet Economics, member of Union of Radical Political Economists, Kalamazoo College, Kalamazoo, Michigan.

The most pressing problem in the former USSR is establishing a market system. In the United States we often identify progressive economic change with regulating markets to improve equity. Given the former USSR's historical absence of a market, progressive economic change there involves establishing fully functioning markets first and regulating markets second.

Although many Soviet economists and policy makers agree that markets should replace the centrally planned system, no clear consensus exists on the new system's form. To me, a market system denotes increased autonomy for the individual to make economic decisions, prices that fluctuate freely, and the chance for people to reap rewards for their economic efforts.

I identify four areas of progressive change that are emerging in the former USSR:

1. Establishing property rights. In the former USSR, consensus now exists to legally guarantee private property rights as the first step in creating a market economy. The republics are discussing three kinds of property rights: the right to own land for private agriculture; the right to own a small business; and the transfer of large industrial enterprises from state ownership to cooperative or private ownership.

The former USSR is already facilitating the growth of small businesses. Called "cooperatives," they run the gamut from single proprietorships to privately owned firms to joint ownership arrangements. But these cooperatives face tremendous obstacles. Cooperative owners must bribe government officials for a multitude of permits, and then must pay protection money to local organized crime.

Despite promises to the contrary, the

former USSR has not enacted legislation enshrining private ownership of land, mainly because deciding on how to distribute land equitably is difficult.

2. Eliminating the system of perquisites. An exclusive economy within the economy provided Party officials with high-quality health care, imported clothing, the best local produce, education, housing, and automobiles. The ordinary citizen didn't know how privileged Party officials were. To achieve a semblance of equity in distribution, this system of perquisites must be eliminated.

3. Allocating resources through a price system. Shortages plagued the economy under central planning. The government attempted to solve this problem with queues and later ration cards. But with the best goods skimmed off for the very few in the Party, the average person's standard of living suffered greatly.

Prices determined solely by supply and demand are the cornerstone of a market economy. The government will have great problems letting prices become free, because prices, particularly food prices, will inevitably increase. Since no one wants to pay more for necessities, and since such price increases hurt those with low incomes the most, the task for Soviet reformers is to find a way to protect low-income people without jeopardizing free prices.

4. Guaranteeing a minimum income. The government would have to finance a minimum income, perhaps by eliminating or reducing military expenditures. Once property rights are established, and producers have the right to set their own prices, prices will reflect supply and demand. Once prices reflect supply and demand, money income will have meaning. Guaranteeing a minimum income will allow people to purchase necessary goods and services.

Mainstream Western academics have a tendency to tell the former USSR to "just have a market," as though markets have no costs or problems, and as though the republics have the institutions to set up a market economy. Without careful thought to establishing checks and balances on business activity, progressive economic change faces an uncertain future. Still, the first task is to set up a market economy. ■

Dollars & Sense, May 1992

Rethinking International Competitiveness

A review of *The Competitive Advantage of Nations* and *The Work of Nations*

By Ronald Kwan

In this election year, concerns over the U.S. economy have taken center stage. But instead of offering constructive ideas, President Bush remains steadfastly laissez-faire, relying on a cyclical economic upturn to aid his reelection bid and North American free trade to restore U.S. competitiveness. Staking their claim to different ground, Democrats, including nominee-apparent Bill Clinton, offer a more interventionist approach to restoring the U.S. economy. For ideas, they—and nervous corporate executives—frequently turn to Harvard professors Michael Porter and Robert Reich.

Unlike laissez-faire economists, Porter and Reich believe a country creates its position in the international economy. Both reject the textbook analysis of trade, which holds a country should let its "comparative advantage" in labor, capital, and natural resources determine what it produces and exports: If Canada has an abundance of natural resources, it should hew wood and draw water for export; Mexico, with its cheap labor, should export labor-intensive products. They reject this, instead offering a choice between low-productivity, low-wage strategies and high-productivity, high-wage ones. To arrive on the high-income side of the divide, Porter and Reich urge countries to invest in education, training, and infrastructure.

But here the two diverge. In *The Competitive Advantage of Nations*, Porter, a member of Ronald Reagan's Commission on Industrial Competitiveness, emphasizes the productivity of firms and the economic environment in which they operate as the keys to national competitiveness. In *The Work of Nations*, Reich, a liberal Bill Clinton adviser, advocates raising the productivity of individuals as the key to attaining a high standard of living. Nonetheless, both believe in the efficiency of the market: Capital should go where it is most profitable and free trade should reign supreme. Countries must make themselves attractive to capital.

But competitiveness, of firms or individuals, is simply not the right goal, because it implies a contest with winners and losers, both between and within countries. High productivity alone does not create a prosperous and democratic society. That depends on how the output

RONALD KWAN is a member of the *Dollars & Sense* Collective and a graduate student in economics at Harvard University.

We cannot expect to find a solution to U.S. economic woes in Reich's policy recommendations since he, like Porter, accepts the global market as efficient.

is distributed. Further, Porter and Reich miss how important communities and a strong labor movement are to a healthy economy.

WINNERS AND LOSERS

Michael Porter asks why, in this era of globalization, are the home bases of internationally competitive firms and industries located in particular countries. He argues that a firm keeps its most productive jobs—those in strategic planning, research and development (R&D), and sophisticated production—at home. Porter claims a nation can attract and hold corporate home bases by providing an environment that encourages innovation. He identifies the key conditions for competitiveness in his "Diamond of National Competitiveness": most important strong domestic rivals that push innovation; clusters of internationally competitive firms, including suppliers; a sophisticated home market that demands the best; and the right labor, natural resources, and infrastructure.

Government policy, according to Porter, should enhance corporate innovation by promoting public and private investments in education and training, physical capital, and a good infrastructure tied to global transportation and communications networks. A far-sighted government will tightly regulate the quality and safety of products and the health of the environment, pushing firms to be competitive in foreign markets that demand higher standards. It will also promote rivalry by deregulating competition, strictly enforcing anti-trust laws, and rejecting managed trade. Ultimately, Porter advises, a firm should look to its bottom line to determine if a country encourages innovation and higher productivity. If not, the firm should find a better home.

The footloose firm is one reason why Robert Reich, who has received favorable attention from some on the left, rejects Porter's notion that core corporations—like General Motors and IBM—make a country competitive. In an argument that's somewhat overdrawn, Reich argues that the firm, as Porter conceives it, no longer exists. According to Reich, decentralized "global webs" have replaced home-based hierarchies. GM, for example, instead of leading a Detroit-centered auto industry, relies on such dispersed strategic planning and R&D that the firm has no real national bonds. Today's corporation will produce where it is cheap, sell where demand is, and do research and planning where the skills are.

What's good for GM, Reich argues, is no longer good for the United States. Of the $20,000 GM receives for a Pontiac Le Mans, Reich notes, $6,000 goes to South Korea for routine labor and assembly, $3,500 to Japan for advanced components (engines, transaxles, and electronics), $1,500 to West Germany for styling and design engineering, about $1,400 to other countries for small components, marketing, and data processing, and some amount to foreign stockholders. Less than $7,600 remains in U.S. hands.

Therefore, Reich is interested not in the competitiveness of firms but in that of individuals. Global capital will hire individuals with skill and insight for high-paying jobs. Reich calls the winners, who are at the top of the income-distribution pyramid, "symbolic analysts"—scientists, engineers, market researchers, entrepreneurs, lawyers, and professors.

THE NATIONAL BARGAIN

In Reich's world, "routine production" workers and "in-person servers" lose. The increased ability of corporations to move operations has eroded labor's bargaining power and fueled a growing gap between rich and poor. U.S. production workers must compete with cheap Third World labor. Wages are bid down and jobs transferred. Retail and fast-food workers lose because production workers must seek service jobs.

Reich recognizes that capital mobility ruptured the national bargain that guided the U.S. economy after World War II. Until the early 1970s, core corporations controlled production and offered good and rising pay—and labor swapped industrial peace for job security and decent wages. Similarly, government did not intrude on corporate decision making, limiting its role to providing education, infrastructure, R&D funds, a market for defense goods, and subsidies for home-buyers. But as transport and communications costs fell, Western Europe and Japan recovered, and more countries entered into high-volume standardized production, competition stiffened and production started moving in pursuit of cheaper labor and resources.

However, since Reich relays a story of responsible corporations and governments, he underplays the role of a strong labor movement and constraints on capital's globalization in striking the bargain. Once controls on capital mobility diminished and government became more anti-union, the balance of power shifted, and unfettered capitalism reasserted itself.

Since Reich doesn't acknowledge the fundamentally adversarial nature of capitalism, he would restore U.S. competitiveness by accommodating global capitalism. To win in the new economy, Reich argues, the U.S. government must make the country attractive global capital—free trade, good infrastructure, and jointly funded basic research. Most important, the country must increase its supply of professionals and highly skilled workers through education and training. Since Reich believes global capitalism can absorb an unlimited number of U.S. symbolic analysts, he argues all Americans can win. (To pay for his programs, Reich recommends cutting defense spending by 50% over the next decade and raising income taxes on the rich to 1977 levels.)

While Porter ignores income distribution, Reich notes the widening income gap and correctly attributes it to global capitalism. Aside from being wealthier than the rest of us and living in splendid isolation, the rich no longer need our labor. In today's economy, the affluent rely on a global rather than national work force. For example, instead of paying union wages to autoworkers in Michigan, carmakers have shifted operations to Mexico and other low-wage havens. This growing gap in interests between wealthy Americans and the rest of the country's citizens explains the affluent's reluctance to fund Reich's strategy.

To get the country back on track, Reich would have us rebuild a national

global mobility of capital does not work. Put simply, when capitalists invest abroad—or threaten to—they often do so seeking lower wages rather than enhanced productivity. Capitalists increase their share of the profits, not the value of production. While both Porter and Reich recommend raising the productivity of Americans through better education and training, so long as capital is free to move, this assault on labor's share will continue.

By wasting resources—like plant and equipment, workers' skills, and public infrastructure—when plants move, capital mobility often reduces efficiency. It would be more productive to create real communities of interest at the plant and

den act as "a potent force toward automation" by pushing firms to innovate and reduce labor costs. We can add that workers accept restructuring because they get high wages, good retraining programs, and a secure social safety net. So it's community, not competition, that is the key to innovation and competitive advantage.

The evidence in Porter's and Reich's books supports the importance of community. But they fail to draw the implication that a coordinated industrial policy can enhance the productivity of the economy. A concerted attempt to improve education and infrastructure and promote cooperation among firms and industries and between workers and employers is the real way to put the economy to work for all of us.

Since capital mobility puts labor at a disadvantage and undermines the creation of a community that can enhance productivity, controls on the international mobility of capital are crucial to developing a functional industrial policy. These might come in the form of employment, training, and reinvestment requirements on firms wishing to invest or sell in a country. But these controls must be multilateral to prevent capital flight.

Because the problem is global capitalism, labor and progressive groups must have a global strategy that incorporates international cooperation and attempts to influence domestic policy in directions of community building. The Canadian Auto Workers union is pursuing such a strategy. Rejecting competitiveness and the impotence Reich attributes to workers, it confronts employers at the plant, industry, and national levels to win changes that promote productivity and a more equitable share of production.

This approach requires, in the workplace and government, the democratic involvement of labor and the recognition and protection of collective bargaining. In short, it requires a political struggle by the people excluded from Reich's and Porter's visions—ordinary working people. ■

The evidence in Porter's and Reich's books supports the importance of community.

community. But he doesn't expect political action from below to bring this about: Production workers and service employees depend too greatly on their superiors to risk offending them. Reich ultimately urges the emergence of a new patriotism and morality so that the winners will care for their fellow citizens. He offers no more promising political agenda.

Reich's plan also rests on dubious economic foundations. He would have the United States multiply the number of symbolic analysts it produces many times over. Assuming such a massive reorientation of the U.S. work force could be carried out, this process—which he notes would not be limited to the United States—would increase the size of the reserve army of professionals, pushing wages down much as globalization has done for production workers.

EFFICIENCY WITH EQUITY

We cannot expect to find a solution to U.S. economic woes in Reich's policy recommendations since he, like Porter, accepts the global market as efficient. But while international economic exchange can advance welfare since countries produce different products, unrestrained

national levels. When workers have a secure job and fair share of the output, they work better and help improve the production process.

Bill Lazonick, an economic historian at Barnard College, attributes the success of 19th-century British manufacturing to communities of craft workers that allowed workers to share in the output, making them willing to train new workers and improve quality and productivity. He attributes the success of large U.S. firms to their creation of communities of managers. These communities of highly valued employees—which did not include production workers—promoted innovation because managers believed they would share in the firm's success.

Lazonick faults Porter's emphasis on competition in R&D. Porter views cooperative research as counterproductive because it reduces the profits of being first. But Lazonick views Porter's clusters of successful firms as communities in which different firms' personnel interact so innovations spread quickly. We can use Lazonick's idea of community to understand and reinterpret other aspects of Porter's work. For example, Porter argues that high wages and benefits in Swe-

RESOURCES: Michael Porter, *The Competitive Advantage of Nations*, Free Press, 1990, $35; Robert Reich, *The Work of Nations: Preparing Ourselves for 21st-Century Capitalism*, Alfred A. Knopf, 1991, $24.

Dollars & Sense, January/February 1993

Happily Never NAFTA

There's no such thing as free trade

By Thea Lee

After deliberating in secret for 14 months, negotiators for the United States, Mexico, and Canada finally unveiled a North American Free Trade Agreement (NAFTA) last September. One thing was immediately apparent to both critics and proponents of the pact: it does not represent classic free trade. Rather, the 2,000-page document orchestrates imports and exports with remarkable attention to detail, and it has as much to do with investment as with trade.

NAFTA is a guide to political and economic clout in North America. The agreement favors multinational corporations and big investors at the expense of workers, farmers, small businesses, and the environment. If ratified by the legislatures of all three countries, NAFTA would hasten the movement of U.S. and Canadian firms to Mexico to profit from cheap labor and lax environmental and workplace regulations.

A fair, humane trade pact would set in motion a process of raising labor and environmental standards for the entire continent. It would not limit the power of domestic governments to regulate trade and investment in the interest of their own countries. If NAFTA meets defeat, the three countries will have a chance to start over, with a more democratic process of negotiation. At the very least, the current agreement could be much improved if citizen groups apply enough pressure. While President-elect Bill Clinton hedged on NAFTA during his campaign, he has indicated willingness to seek substantial reforms.

MORE JOBS

Much of the debate over NAFTA concerns employment. "Jobs, jobs, jobs," promised Carla Hills, the U.S. Trade Representative, at the Republican Convention. Proponents of free trade argue that it fosters growth by removing artificial barriers, thus rewarding efficient firms. All nations benefit. Without tariffs and subsidies, countries specialize in goods they make relatively cheaply. Higher efficiency means lower prices, so workers see their purchasing power grow. While some people lose their jobs in the shakeup that follows newly liberalized trade, other jobs open in expanding industries. In the case of North America, by further opening Mexico's consumer market to imports, NAFTA will supposedly create hundreds of thousands of export-related jobs in the United States and Canada.

So the theory goes. In the real world, however, the touted benefits won't necessarily come to pass. In the absence of full employment, for example, displaced workers don't automatically find new jobs at comparable wages. Unemployment currently runs at about 20% in Mexico, 11% in Canada, and 7.5% in the United States.

According to the U.S. Bureau of Labor Statistics, displaced American manufac-turing workers who find new jobs take an average 10% pay cut, after accounting for inflation.

Second, lower costs don't necessarily translate into lower prices. NAFTA would allow already huge U.S. corporations to expand their share of the Mexican market. As they drive small Mexican firms out of business, multinationals would face dwindling competition. Therefore, they will not necessarily face pressure to pass cost savings to consumers dollar for dollar.

And as for efficiency, it's not much to get excited about when the savings come from cheap labor rather than better technology or easier access to resources. In fact, as firms shift production to Mexico, lured by wages of $1 or $2 an hour, they lose some incentive to invest in cutting-edge techniques that improve productivity. For years, U.S. firms have been setting up "maquiladora" factories just over the Mexican border, and NAFTA would simply speed the trend.

Given such contradictory visions of free trade, it's no surprise that competing studies of NAFTA predict contrasting results. Proponents forecast job and wage gains in all three countries, while critics predict wage erosion and job losses for Canada and the United States, with small gains for a minority of Mexicans.

Some difference of opinion over NAFTA's impact is legitimate. Reasonable people might disagree about how many U.S. and Canadian companies would shift production to Mexico, for instance. But for the most part, the debate in political circles hasn't been reasonable at all. Virtually all of the models predicting job gains for the United States are disingenuous. They focus solely on lower trade barriers, ignoring the shift in investment from north to south. The Bush administration has consistently cited studies that are even less realistic, including one by the Peat Marwick accounting firm and another done jointly by researchers at the University of Michigan and Tufts University. These studies acknowledge that investment will increase in Mexico, but they assume no corresponding loss in the United States. That's equivalent to assuming that Mexicans will wake up one morning to find an extra $25 billion in the middle of Main Street.

THEA LEE, a former *D&S* editor, is an economist at the Economic Policy Institute in Washington, D C.

When the likely shift in investment is correctly taken into account, most models do show a net job loss for the United States. For example, research by the Economic Policy Institute, a Washington think tank, and a study by economists at Skidmore College and the University of Massachusetts at Amherst suggest NAFTA would cost the United States at least half a million jobs over the next decade. That's less than 0.5% of the total U.S. workforce, but the decline would likely be sharp in several industries, including apparel, autos and auto parts, consumer electronics, and food processing. The loss, or even the threat of it, would be enough to reduce wages across much of the labor force. U.S. wages and benefits are seven times higher than Mexico's on average, and the gap is much wider in some occupations. Professor Ed Leamer of the University of California at Los Angeles predicts a loss of about $1,000 a year per person for approximately 70% of the U.S. work force—everyone but managers, scientists, and technicians.

If Canada's experience with free trade offers any lessons, the prospects for the United States look grim. Canada has lost almost a quarter of its manufacturing jobs since it entered into a free trade agreement with the United States in 1989. And Canadian wages are only slightly higher than in the United States. While the agreement is only partly to blame, proponents of that pact, too, promised job gains for Canada. As it turned out, hundreds of plants left Canada for the United States in pursuit of labor savings, lower taxes, and cheaper real estate. A depreciated U.S. dollar also fueled the flight.

A recent *Wall Street Journal* poll of U.S. corporate executives found that 40% have plans to move some production to Mexico in the near future. Twenty-five percent admitted that they plan to use the threat of moving as a bargaining chip to cut wages and benefits.

DUBIOUS GAINS FOR MEXICO

NAFTA locks Mexico into a dead-end development strategy: attracting foreign investment with low wages, weak unions, and toothless regulations. While U.S. multinationals would bring new manufacturing jobs to Mexico, these gains will not be large enough to employ all the new entrants into the labor force. The country's labor force is growing rapidly, due to a burgeoning population and a massive number of youth who are coming of age. Thus, continuing high unemployment and underemployment will likely maintain downward pressure on wages. Mexico's minimum wage has already fallen by almost 50% since the early 1980s, after accounting for inflation. The country is already suffering from growing unemployment, massive debt, and an anti-labor government.

In addition, losses in farming and small business would offset some of the new factory jobs, as huge corporations and agribusiness consolidate power and find ways to save on labor. Domestic production of U.S. and Canadian transnationals would drive some small entrepreneurs out of business. So would cheap imports. Despite low labor costs, some protected Mexican industries are ill-prepared to meet new competition from abroad because they don't have up-to-date facilities. Lifting subsidies and tariffs in agriculture would likely give Mexico an advantage over the United States in fruits and vegetables. But the United States stands to gain in corn, grain, and beans. NAFTA could spur improvements in agricultural productivity, but farmers shouldn't have to bear the entire burden of adjustment.

LABOR AND ENVIRONMENTAL STANDARDS

NAFTA is silent on the disparate labor laws, wages, and working conditions among the three signatory countries. The agreement stands in sad contrast to the integration plan of the European Community, which is trying to set minimum job standards and benefits, so that countries can't compete by pummeling workers. The EC's more just plan reflects the way it was negotiated: publicly, with more democratic participation and an explicit concern for workers' rights. NAFTA negotiators, on the other hand, have virtually guaranteed that competition will debase the standards of countries that now offer the best protection.

Mexico has lenient child labor laws, and they aren't well enforced. 14- and 15-year-olds are allowed to work up to 36 hours a week, while the U.S. limit is 18 hours during school season. Children make up almost one-third of Mexico's work force, according to the Mexican Center for Children's Rights.

Mexican labor laws are better than the United States' in many areas, such as maternity leave. But they are poorly enforced. The Mexican constitution protects the right to bargain collectively and to strike. In practice, however, the largest Mexican unions are allied with the ruling political party, the Independent Revolutionary Party (PRI). The government may declare a strike illegal, allowing the company to fire strikers.

NAFTA should require all countries to meet the highest labor standards now in place in any of the three nations. To enforce those standards, workers and unions should have the right to challenge the import of goods produced in a way that violates standards of their own country.

NAFTA would be a big step backward from current U.S. trade law, which at least nominally protects worker rights. Under certain trade agreements, such as the Caribbean Basin Initiative, the United States must allow workers to bargain collectively and must set certain minimum standards for pay, hours, and workplace health and safety. These trade agreements also prohibit forced labor and limit child labor. While enforcement often falls short, these laws provide leverage in putting a stop to some of the worst abuses.

NAFTA offers a bit more protection to the environment than to workers, but not much. William Reilly of the U.S. Environmental Protection Agency has called NAFTA the "greenest trade agreement ever negotiated," referring to a clause that supposedly prevents countries from relaxing their health, safety, or environmental standards to attract foreign investment. But the text does not actually prohibit such a move, only deems it "inappropriate." The penalty for violation? The injured party could "request consultations" but could impose no legal sanction. Ouch. In addition, NAFTA states that technical standards imposed by the pact refer only to the end product, not the way products are made. So an electrical appliance maker that dumped toxic waste into a Mexican stream could freely export "safe" products to the United States or Canada.

INVESTMENT

While NAFTA all but ignores labor standards, it devotes five out of 22 chapters to investment. The text is designed to foster corporate mobility, to make it as easy for a U.S. company to operate in Matamoros, Mexico as in Milwaukee. In the process, the pact invades territory traditionally reserved for domestic policy, in order to promote and protect the interests of investors. All three countries would sign away important tools of economic policy.

For example, given Mexico's history of nationalizing private businesses, a potential investor might worry about a government takeover. Article 1110 would put that fear to rest, restricting expropriation to certain circumstances and specifying the compensation, currency, and interest rate that would apply in the event of nationalization.

The cautious investor might also fret about limits on exchanging pesos for dollars, or a requirement to reinvest some profits locally. Not to worry. Article 1109 would mandate that all transfers of business income shall "be made freely and without delay" and would prohibit any of the three countries from requiring domestic reinvestment of profits.

Under Article 1106, none of the three countries could require a company's exports to match or exceed its imports, as Mexico currently does for autos. The article rules out other national policies that would foster domestic development, like requiring foreign-based firms to buy domestic supplies, hire local scientists and managers, or make technology available to domestic firms. Such requirements have to date been routine in Europe, Mexico, and Canada.

This article even goes so far as to apply to countries outside the pact. This provision says that the United States, for instance, couldn't require Japanese auto plants producing in the United States to buy a certain number of parts from domestic suppliers or to transfer technology. Those are policies the United States has so far failed to pursue, but should have the option to at least consider.

NAFTA would also thwart domestic policy in the area of intellectual property rights, that is, copyrights and patents on printed material, sound or video recordings, pharmaceuticals, and computer software. Developing nations often show little regard for intellectual property rights, since exclusive authority to make a product generally means steep prices. By ignoring drug patents, for example, Mexico has provided relatively cheap pharmaceuticals.

No longer. The U.S. trade representative boasts that "NAFTA provides a higher standard of protection for patents, copyrights, trademarks, and trade secrets than has been established in any other bilateral or international agreement." For pharmaceutical and agricultural chemical companies, NAFTA offers an opportunity to exert long-sought control over other countries. The Mexican government is willing to make this sacrifice in exchange for access to the markets of industrialized countries. But the tradeoff enhances corporate profits while imposing higher costs on consumers in poor countries. Even Canadians would pay more for pharmaceuticals under NAFTA, since Canada limits patent rights more than the United States does. NAFTA would cost Canada an extra $400 million a year in higher drug prices.

NAFTA includes elaborate provisions for resolving disputes, calling for arbitration by a panel of international trade lawyers and financial "experts" appointed by the executive branch. Like NAFTA in general, the proposed penalties for violations put property before people. Madonna's record company could seek lost profits and legal fees from anyone who made unauthorized copies of her cassettes. The offending tapes and the factory used to make them could be confiscated. Yet, since NAFTA imposes almost no labor standards, it offers no way to block U.S. imports of clothing made by a Mexican company that exploits child labor.

WHAT TO DO

With enough pressure on political leaders in all three countries, NAFTA could be rejected, or at least reformed substantially. While the pact will probably sail through the Mexican Senate with little debate, it faces strong opposition in Canada and the United States. Canada's recent free trade pact with the U.S. is unpopular, and Canadians don't consider NAFTA much better. Prime Minister Brian Mulroney faces serious political risk in pushing the agreement through Parliament before the next election.

Before he was elected, Bill Clinton criticized NAFTA for omitting labor and environmental standards. Yet he said he favored free trade with Mexico in principle and thought the pact could be fixed without renegotiating the basic agreement.

He faces a skeptical public. Bush's resounding defeat at the polls was a pretty clear indicator that, with unemployment stuck at 7.5%, most people are looking for a more plausible jobs bill than this one. A CBS-New York Times poll in July found that Americans thought NAFTA was a "bad idea" by a 2-to-1 margin. Another poll cited by the Los Angeles Times in September found only 16% of the population believed NAFTA would create jobs in the United States.

Citizen groups are pressing for a pact that provides for labor and environmental standards no weaker than the strongest now in force in North America. The standards should be enforceable through trade sanctions, not simply encouraged by an advisory commission. The agreement should provide for money to clean up pollution and aid displaced workers. That's a costly proposition, and the companies that benefit from transnational trade and investment should pay. U.S. Rep. Richard Gephardt (D-Missouri) has suggested a tax along these lines, which he calls a "cross-border transaction fee."

A renegotiation of NAFTA should be open to democratic participation by labor, environmental, farming, and consumer groups. It's possible to manage trade in the interest of working people and the environment. ■

Resources: Jeff Faux and Thea Lee, "The Effect of George Bush's NAFTA on American Workers: Ladder Up or Ladder Down?" Washington, D.C., Economic Policy Institute (EPI), July 1992, 800 537-9359. Robert Blecker and William Spriggs, "Manufacturing Employment in North America: Where the Jobs Have Gone," EPI, October 1992. Tim Koechlin and Mehrene Larudee, "The High Cost of NAFTA," *Challenge*, September/October 1992. Labor Advisory Committee on the NAFTA, "Preliminary Report," September 16, 1992.

economy in numbers

Dollars & Sense, July/August 1992

U.S. among worst in inequality

Among 21 top industrialized countries, only Australia has a higher rate of income inequality than the United States, according to recently published figures from the United Nations Development Programme (UNDP).

For 21 countries that had the highest rankings on the UNDP's "Human Development Index," a measure of social and economic well-being, the United States finished next to worst by two measures:

• The richest 20% of U.S. households make about 10 times as much as the poorest 20%.

• The poorest 40% of U.S. households earn only 16% of national income.

Former Eastern Bloc nations Hungary and Poland performed best on equality, but such capitalist powerhouses as Japan and Germany were also far more egalitarian than the United States. The gap between the top and bottom Japanese households was less than half as wide as in the United States. The lowest 40% of Japanese households received about one-third more of the national income than the same group here.

The data shown in the table must be regarded with some caution. They are for varying years between 1980-88 depending on the country, and the quality of the data varies from one nation to another.

The gap between rich and poor Americans is not only large, it's also growing. Between 1983 and 1989, according to U.S. government sources, the share of total wealth owned by the top one-half of one percent (0.5%) of U.S. households increased from 24% to 29%.

Lower earnings among workers go a long way toward explaining income inequality. According to the Census Bureau, between 1979 and 1989, the percent of full-time, year-round employees earning "low wages," defined as less than $12,195 a year, increased from 12% to 18% of the total work force.

The rise in low-wage workers took place mainly among men, whose percent rose from 13% to 18%. Rates for women were much higher than for men in both years but stayed relatively constant, varying from 29% in 1979 to 30% in 1989. The percentage earning low wages rose substantially for Latinos, from 30% to 37%, and for whites, from 11% to 16%, but stayed approximately constant for African-Americans, going from 30.5% to 31.0%.

One popular explanation among mainstream economists for wage rates is worker productivity. Yet, at least in manufacturing, productivity trends fail to explain what has happened to U.S. wages in recent years. According to a study by Andrew Sum of Northeastern University, from 1979 through 1989 real hourly earnings for manufacturing workers fell by 8.3%, despite growth in output per hour of 26.3%. This contrasts sharply with the three previous decades. Productivity rose by around 30% a decade from the 1950s through the 1970s. In the 1950s wage gains were slightly greater than productivity increases, but in the 1960s wages rose by only half as much as productivity. And in the 1970s wages rose only 6.1%.

RESOURCES: United Nations Development Programme, *Human Development Report*, 1992; U.S. Bureau of the Census, "Workers with Low Earnings: 1964-1990," May 1992; *Business Week*, "Would the Economy Gain From Spreading Inherited Wealth?" May 18, 1992; Andrew Sum, "Broken Promises: Rising Labor Productivity in Manufacturing and the Decline in the Real Earnings of Production Workers Over the 1979-1989 Period," Northeastern University Center for Labor Market Studies, 1992.

Rankings of income inequality

For industrialized nations, 1980-1988

	Ratio of highest 20% to lowest 20%	Income share of lowest 40%
Hungary	3.0	26.2
Poland	3.6	23.9
Japan	4.3	21.9
Sweden	4.6	21.2
Belgium	4.6	21.6
Netherlands	5.6	20.1
Germany*	5.7	19.5
Spain	5.8	19.4
Norway	5.9	19.0
Finland	6.0	18.4
Italy	6.0	18.8
France	6.5	18.4
Israel	6.6	18.1
United Kingdom	6.8	17.3
Yugoslavia	7.0	17.1
Canada	7.1	17.5
Denmark	7.1	17.4
Switzerland	8.6	16.9
New Zealand	8.8	15.9
United States	8.9	15.7
Australia	9.6	15.5

*Former East Germany not included.